GCSE AQA A
Core Science
Foundation — the Basics
The Revision Guide

This book is for anyone doing **GCSE AQA A Core Science**
at Foundation Level, with a predicted grade of D or below.
(If you're not sure what your predicted grade is, your teacher will be able to tell you.)

All the important topics are explained in a clear, straightforward
way to help you get all the marks you can in the exam.

And of course, there are some daft bits to make the whole
thing vaguely entertaining for you.

<u>What CGP is all about</u>

Our sole aim here at CGP is to produce the highest
quality books — carefully written, immaculately presented
and dangerously close to being funny.

Then we work our socks off to get them out to you — at the cheapest possible prices.

Contents

CHEMISTRY 1B — OILS, EARTH AND ATMOSPHERE

PHYSICS 1A — ENERGY

PHYSICS 1B — ELECTRICITY AND WAVES

Published by CGP

Editors:
Ellen Bowness, Charlotte Burrows, Katherine Craig, Emma Elder, Mary Falkner,
Helena Hayes, Felicity Inkpen, Rosie McCurrie, Edmund Robinson, Helen Ronan,
Jane Sawers, Sarah Williams and Dawn Wright.

ISBN: 978 1 84762 710 0

With thanks to Hayley Thompson and Karen Wells for the proofreading.

With thanks to Jeremy Cooper, Janet Cruse-Sawyer, Ian Francis and Jamie Sinclair for the reviewing.

With thanks to Jan Greenway, Laura Jakubowski and Laura Stoney for the copyright research.

With thanks to Science Photo Library for permission to use the image on page 29.

Groovy website: www.cgpbooks.co.uk

Printed by Elanders Ltd, Newcastle upon Tyne.
Jolly bits of clipart from CorelDRAW®

Based on the classic CGP style created by Richard Parsons.

Photocopying — it's dull, grey and sometimes a bit naughty. Luckily, it's dead cheap, easy and quick to order
more copies of this book from CGP — just call us on 0870 750 1242. Phew!

The Exams

You need to know what exams you're taking and <u>what to learn</u> for each one.
...s <u>really important</u>. So read on...

There are Different Parts to GCSE Science

1) In your exams you'll be tested on <u>Biology</u>, <u>Chemistry</u> and <u>Physics</u>. These are all covered in this book.

2) You need to know about <u>How Science Works</u> too. There's a <u>whole section</u> on this — see pages 2-9.

3) You also have to do a <u>Controlled Assessment</u> (also known as an 'ISA') — it's a bit like a <u>coursework exam</u>. You'll do the Controlled Assessment in <u>class</u>.

There are Two Different Sets of Exams You Could Do

There are <u>two different ways</u> you can be tested for GCSE Science — <u>Route 1</u> and <u>Route 2</u>.
Your <u>teacher</u> will be able to tell you which one you're doing.

If You're Doing Route 1...

You'll have to do <u>three</u> exams...

1) The <u>Unit 1 exam</u> tests you on <u>BIOLOGY</u>.
You need to revise <u>Sections B1a and B1b</u> of this book for this exam.

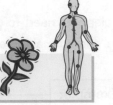

2) The <u>Unit 2 exam</u> tests you on <u>CHEMISTRY</u>.
You need to revise <u>Sections C1a and C1b</u> of this book for this exam.

3) The <u>Unit 3 exam</u> tests you on <u>PHYSICS</u>.
You need to revise <u>Sections P1a and P1b</u> of this book for this exam.

You also have to do a <u>Controlled Assessment</u> (ISA).

If You're Doing Route 2...

You'll have to do <u>two</u> exams...

1) The <u>Unit 5 exam</u> tests you on <u>BIOLOGY</u>, <u>CHEMISTRY</u> and <u>PHYSICS</u>.
You need to revise <u>Sections B1a</u>, <u>C1a</u> and <u>P1a</u> of this book for this exam.

2) The <u>Unit 6 exam</u> tests you on <u>BIOLOGY</u>, <u>CHEMISTRY</u> and <u>PHYSICS</u> as well.
You need to revise <u>Sections B1b</u>, <u>C1b</u> and <u>P1b</u> of this book for this exam.

You also have to do a <u>Controlled Assessment</u> (ISA).

The Scientific Process

For your <u>exams</u> and your <u>controlled assessment</u>, you need to know how the world of science <u>works</u>.

A Hypothesis is an Explanation of Something

1) Scientists <u>OBSERVE</u> (look at) things they <u>don't understand</u>.

2) They then come up with an <u>explanation</u> for what they've seen.

3) This explanation is called a <u>HYPOTHESIS</u>.

> **For Example:**
>
> A scientist is looking at <u>why</u> people have <u>spots</u>.
>
> He notices that everyone with spots <u>picks their nose</u>.
>
> The scientist thinks that the spots might be <u>caused</u> by people picking their nose.
>
>
>
> Nose picking = spots?
>
>
>
> So the <u>hypothesis</u> is: **"Spots are caused by picking your nose."**

4) Next, scientists need to <u>check</u> whether the <u>hypothesis</u> is <u>RIGHT or NOT</u>.

5) They do this by making a <u>PREDICTION</u> and <u>TESTING</u> it.

> **For Example:**
>
> A prediction is something like: **"People who pick their nose will have spots."**

Sometimes a hypothesis and a prediction are the same thing.

6) If tests show that the <u>prediction</u> is <u>RIGHT</u>, then there's <u>EVIDENCE</u> (signs) that the <u>hypothesis is right</u> too.

7) If tests show that the <u>prediction</u> is <u>WRONG</u>, then the <u>hypothesis</u> is probably <u>wrong</u> as well.

Other Scientists Test the Hypothesis by Making Predictions

1) It's <u>NOT enough</u> for <u>one scientist</u> to do tests to see if the hypothesis is right or not.

2) <u>Other scientists</u> test the hypothesis as well.

3) Sometimes these scientists will find <u>more evidence</u> that the <u>hypothesis is RIGHT</u>.

4) When this happens the hypothesis is <u>accepted</u> and goes into <u>books</u> for people to learn.

New science stuff to learn

I agree...

5) Sometimes the scientists will find <u>evidence</u> that shows the <u>hypothesis is WRONG</u>.

6) When this happens the scientists have to start <u>all over again</u>. Sad times.

Investigations

To find out <u>how things work</u>, <u>what causes something</u>, or <u>whether something is true</u>, scientists carry out investigations. You'll also have to carry out investigations — so you need to know what they're all about.

Investigations Give Us Evidence

1) To <u>find stuff out</u>, scientists carry out <u>INVESTIGATIONS</u>.

2) Investigations give scientists <u>EVIDENCE</u> to <u>back up their ideas</u>.

3) Evidence is <u>really important</u>. Without it all you've got is an <u>opinion</u>. And that doesn't count for much.

4) You can do investigations in a <u>lab</u> or <u>somewhere else</u>. It depends on <u>what</u> you're investigating. For example...

A <u>lab</u> is the best place to study cells using a microscope.

But if you're studying what kinds of rabbits are found in a <u>wood</u> you'll need to go to the <u>wood</u>.

Investigations Have to be Fair Tests

1) When you <u>plan</u> an investigation you need to make sure it will be a **FAIR TEST**.

2) To make an investigation fair you must...

ONLY CHANGE ONE THING. EVERYTHING ELSE must be kept the SAME.

3) The thing that you <u>CHANGE</u> is called the <u>INDEPENDENT</u> variable.

4) The things that you <u>keep the SAME</u> are called <u>CONTROL</u> variables.

5) The thing that's <u>MEASURED</u> is called the <u>DEPENDENT</u> variable.

Example: Investigation to see how changing the <u>amount of light</u> changes <u>how tall a plant grows</u>

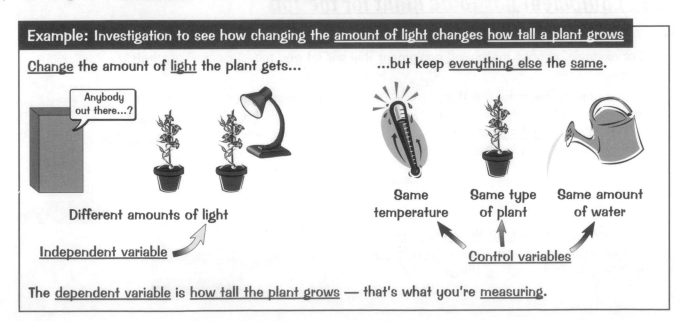

<u>Change</u> the amount of <u>light</u> the plant gets...

...but keep <u>everything else</u> the <u>same</u>.

Anybody out there...?

Different amounts of light

Independent variable

Same temperature

Same type of plant

Same amount of water

Control variables

The <u>dependent variable</u> is <u>how tall the plant grows</u> — that's what you're <u>measuring</u>.

How Science Works

Investigations

More stuff on investigations coming up on this page. This time it's about <u>how many</u> things you should test (the <u>sample size</u>) and what <u>equipment</u> you should use. All mighty important stuff.

The Bigger the Sample Size the Better

1) Sample size is <u>how MANY things are in the group you're testing</u>. For example, how many <u>plants</u> you test, or how many <u>people</u>.

2) The <u>BIGGER</u> the sample size the <u>BETTER</u>.

3) But scientists have to be <u>sensible</u> when choosing how big their sample should be.

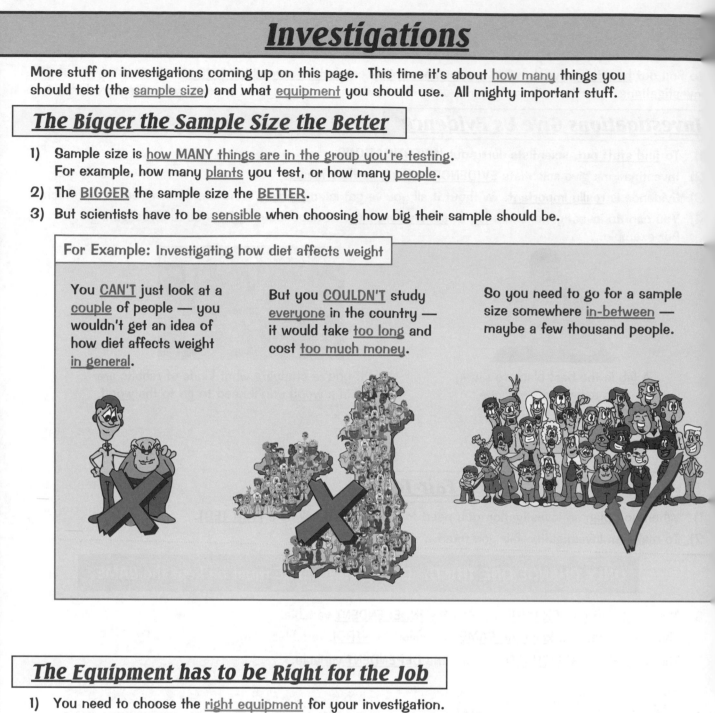

For Example: Investigating how diet affects weight

You <u>CAN'T</u> just look at a <u>couple</u> of people — you wouldn't get an idea of how diet affects weight <u>in general</u>.

But you <u>COULDN'T</u> study <u>everyone</u> in the country — it would take <u>too long</u> and cost <u>too much money</u>.

So you need to go for a sample size somewhere <u>in-between</u> — maybe a few thousand people.

The Equipment has to be Right for the Job

1) You need to choose the <u>right equipment</u> for your investigation.

2) For example, choose <u>measuring equipment</u> that will let you measure stuff <u>accurately</u>.

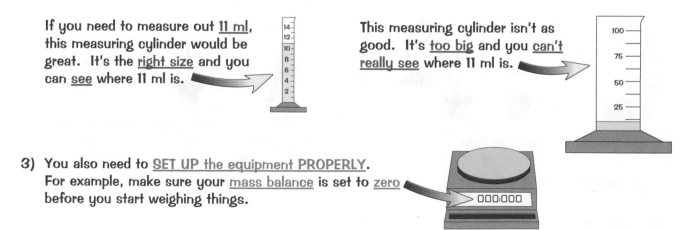

If you need to measure out <u>11 ml</u>, this measuring cylinder would be great. It's the <u>right size</u> and you can <u>see</u> where 11 ml is.

This measuring cylinder isn't as good. It's <u>too big</u> and you <u>can't really see</u> where 11 ml is.

3) You also need to <u>SET UP the equipment PROPERLY</u>. For example, make sure your <u>mass balance</u> is set to <u>zero</u> before you start weighing things.

Investigations

On to the <u>dangers</u> of investigations now, and how to make sure your results are <u>reliable</u>.

Investigations Can be Dangerous

1) A <u>HAZARD</u> is something that <u>could cause HARM</u>.

2) Hazards include things like...

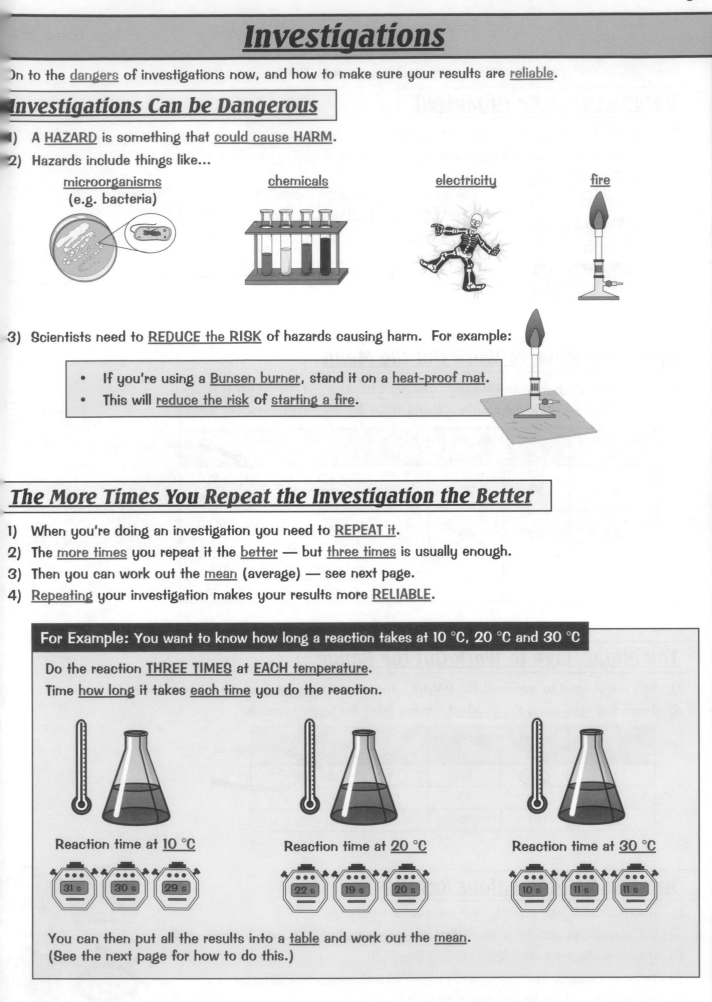

microorganisms
(e.g. bacteria)

chemicals

electricity

fire

3) Scientists need to <u>REDUCE the RISK</u> of hazards causing harm. For example:

- If you're using a <u>Bunsen burner</u>, stand it on a <u>heat-proof mat</u>.
- This will <u>reduce the risk</u> of <u>starting a fire</u>.

The More Times You Repeat the Investigation the Better

1) When you're doing an investigation you need to <u>REPEAT it</u>.

2) The <u>more times</u> you repeat it the <u>better</u> — but <u>three times</u> is usually enough.

3) Then you can work out the <u>mean</u> (average) — see next page.

4) <u>Repeating</u> your investigation makes your results more <u>RELIABLE</u>.

For Example: You want to know how long a reaction takes at 10 °C, 20 °C and 30 °C

Do the reaction <u>THREE TIMES</u> at <u>EACH</u> temperature.
Time <u>how long</u> it takes <u>each time</u> you do the reaction.

Reaction time at <u>10 °C</u>

Reaction time at <u>20 °C</u>

Reaction time at <u>30 °C</u>

| 31 s | 30 s | 29 s |

| 22 s | 19 s | 20 s |

| 10 s | 11 s | 11 s |

You can then put all the results into a <u>table</u> and work out the <u>mean</u>.
(See the next page for how to do this.)

Organising Data

Once you've collected your data it needs to be <u>organised</u>. The fun doesn't stop...

Data Needs to be Organised

1) <u>TABLES</u> are dead useful for <u>organising data</u>.

2) Make sure that <u>each column</u> has a <u>HEADING</u> and that you've put the <u>UNITS</u> in.

Temperature (°C)	Repeat 1 (s)	Repeat 2 (s)	Repeat 3 (s)
10	31	30	29
20	22	19	20
30	10	11	11

Column headings
Units

You Might Have to Work Out the Mean

1) If you've <u>repeated</u> an investigation you need to work out the <u>MEAN</u> (average).

2) Just <u>ADD TOGETHER</u> the results. Then <u>DIVIDE</u> by the total number of results.

Temperature (°C)	Repeat 1 (s)	Repeat 2 (s)	Repeat 3 (s)	Mean (s)
10	31	30	29	$\frac{(31 + 30 + 29) = 30}{3}$
20	22	19	20	$\frac{(22 + 19 + 20) = 20.3}{3}$
30	10	11	11	$\frac{(10 + 11 + 11) = 10.7}{3}$

Add together the results

Divide by 3 (because there are three results for 10 °C)

You Might Have to Work Out the Range

1) You might need to work out the <u>RANGE</u>. The range is <u>how spread out</u> the results are.

2) To do this <u>take away</u> the <u>smallest</u> number from the <u>biggest</u> number.

Temperature (°C)	Repeat 1 (s)	Repeat 2 (s)	Repeat 3 (s)	Range(s)
10	(31)	30	(29)	31 - 29 = 2
20	22	19	20	22 - 19 = 3
30	10	11	11	11 - 10 = 1

Biggest number at 10 °C
Smallest number at 10 °C

You Can Get Anomalous Results

1) The results of your investigation will always <u>vary a bit</u>.

2) But sometimes you get a result that <u>doesn't seem to FIT IN</u> with the rest at all.

3) These results are called <u>ANOMALOUS RESULTS</u>.

4) You can <u>IGNORE</u> them when you're working out <u>means</u> and <u>ranges</u>.

5) But you should try to find out what <u>caused them</u>.

Anomalous result

Presenting Data

Scientists just love presenting data as graphs (weirdos)...

Bar Charts are Used When You've Got Categories

1) CATEGORIES are things like blood type or ice cream flavour. You can't get results in-between categories.

2) If you're measuring something that comes in categories you should use a BAR chart to show the data.

3) There are some rules you need to follow for drawing bar charts...

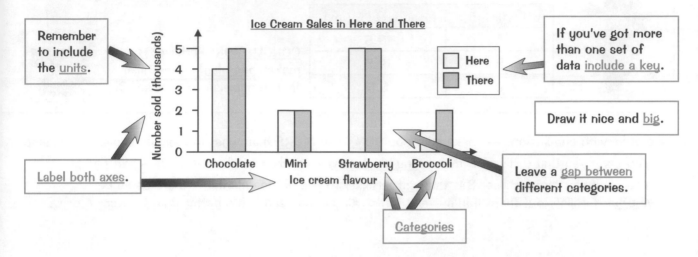

Remember to include the units.

Label both axes.

If you've got more than one set of data include a key.

Draw it nice and big.

Leave a gap between different categories.

Categories

You Need to be Able to Draw Line Graphs

1) If you're measuring something that can have ANY value you should use a LINE graph to show the data.

2) For example, temperatures and people's heights would be shown using a line graph.

3) Here are the rules for drawing line graphs...

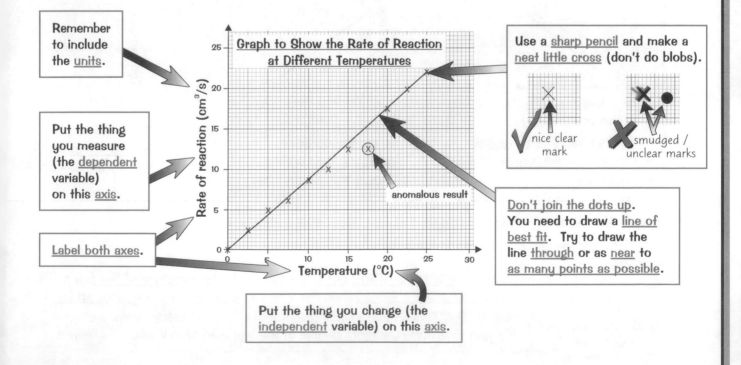

Remember to include the units.

Put the thing you measure (the dependent variable) on this axis.

Label both axes.

Use a sharp pencil and make a neat little cross (don't do blobs).

nice clear mark

smudged / unclear marks

anomalous result

Don't join the dots up. You need to draw a line of best fit. Try to draw the line through or as near to as many points as possible.

Put the thing you change (the independent variable) on this axis.

How Science Works

Drawing Conclusions

So, you've organised and presented your data. Next thing to do is to write a <u>conclusion</u>.

You Can Only Conclude What the Data Shows and NO MORE

To come to a conclusion, <u>look at your data</u> and <u>say what pattern you see</u>.

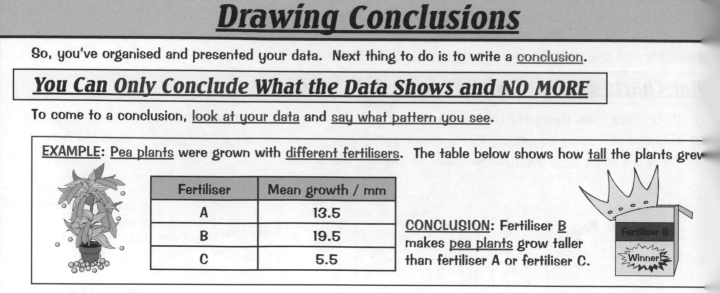

<u>EXAMPLE</u>: <u>Pea plants</u> were grown with <u>different fertilisers</u>. The table below shows how <u>tall</u> the plants grew.

Fertiliser	Mean growth / mm
A	13.5
B	19.5
C	5.5

<u>CONCLUSION</u>: Fertiliser <u>B</u> makes <u>pea plants</u> grow taller than fertiliser A or fertiliser C.

Fertiliser B
Winner!

Be careful with conclusions — make sure you <u>DON'T</u> say <u>MORE</u> than what the results show. For example...

- You <u>can't</u> say that fertiliser B makes <u>any plant</u> grow taller than fertiliser A or C — just <u>pea plants</u>.
- You <u>can't</u> say that fertiliser B is the <u>best</u> fertiliser to use on pea plants — there could be <u>another fertiliser</u> out there that's <u>even better</u>. All you can say is it's <u>better than fertiliser A or C</u>.

Line Graphs Show Patterns in Data

1) Line graphs are great for <u>showing the relationship</u> (the link) between two things.

2) The relationship is called a <u>CORRELATION</u>. You need to know about <u>three types of correlation</u>...

POSITIVE CORRELATION

As one thing <u>increases</u> so does the other.

Temperature

Bottles of sun cream sold

As the <u>temperature increases</u> the amount of <u>sun cream</u> sold also <u>increases</u>.

NEGATIVE CORRELATION

As one thing <u>increases</u> the other <u>decreases</u>.

Temperature

Woolly hats sold

As the <u>temperature increases</u> the number of <u>hats</u> sold <u>decreases</u>.

NO CORRELATION

There's <u>no relationship</u> between the two things.

Temperature

Bread sold

The temperature has <u>no effect</u> on the amount of bread sold.

3) Even if there <u>IS</u> a <u>correlation</u>, it <u>DOESN'T</u> always mean that a change in one thing is <u>CAUSING</u> the change in the other. For example...

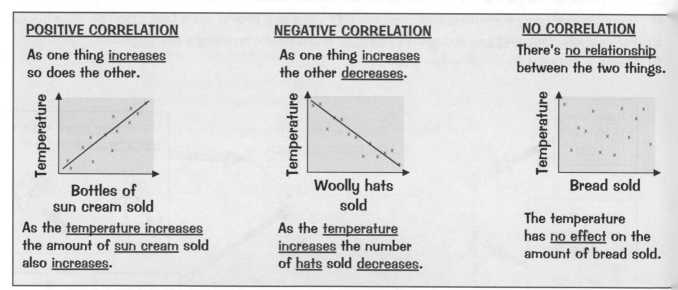

Temperature

Number of shark attacks

- There's a <u>POSITIVE CORRELATION</u> between the <u>temperature of the sea</u> and the <u>number of shark attacks</u> (when the water is <u>warmer</u> there are <u>more attacks</u>).
- This <u>DOESN'T</u> mean that sharks are more likely to attack in warm water — it's just that there are <u>more people in the water</u> to attack when it's warm.

Bias and Problems

There's more to science than doing experiments and collecting data. There are always <u>problems</u> to sort out.

Scientific Evidence can be Biased

1) Sometimes people try to <u>AFFECT</u> how others <u>think</u>.

2) They do this by <u>showing data</u> in a <u>certain way</u>. For example...

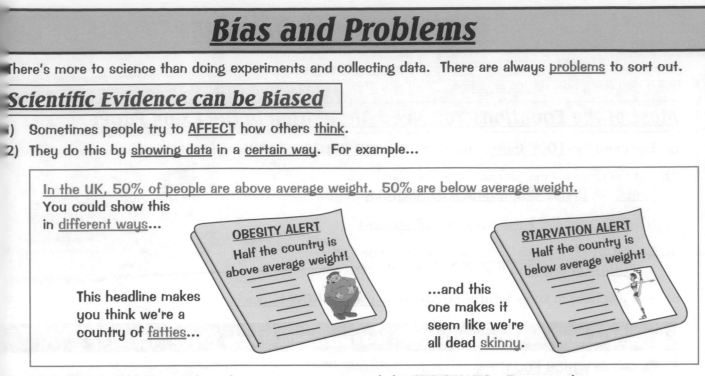

In the UK, 50% of people are above average weight. 50% are below average weight.
You could show this in <u>different ways</u>...

OBESITY ALERT
Half the country is above average weight!

This headline makes you think we're a country of <u>fatties</u>...

...and this one makes it seem like we're all dead <u>skinny</u>.

STARVATION ALERT
Half the country is below average weight!

3) Sometimes people try to show data in a certain way to <u>help THEMSELVES</u>. For example...

- <u>Governments</u> want to make people <u>vote</u> for them.
- <u>Companies</u> want to make their products sound <u>better</u>.

4) When this happens you <u>can't always trust</u> what they say — we say they are <u>BIASED</u>.

Scientific Developments can Cause Problems

Science is <u>really useful</u>. For example, we have <u>better medicines</u> and <u>new technology</u> because of science. But it can cause <u>problems</u>. For example...

Economic (money) problems:

Governments <u>can't</u> always <u>afford</u> to do the things that scientists think they should.

Social (people) problems:

Some decisions affect <u>PEOPLE</u>. For example, science has shown that <u>drinking too much alcohol</u> is bad for your health. But lots of people <u>wouldn't like it</u> if alcohol was <u>banned</u>.

Ethical (moral) problems:

Just because we <u>CAN</u> do something doesn't mean that we <u>should</u>. For example, we <u>can</u> make <u>more nuclear weapons</u>, but lots of people think that it's <u>wrong</u>.

No More Nukes!

Environmental problems:

Sometimes new science developments can <u>DAMAGE the environment</u>.

How Science Works

Using Equations

Sometimes in science you have to do some maths. Boo. Hiss.
But if you learn how to use equations, they're a great way to pick up marks in the exam.

Most of the Equations You Need Are Written in the Exam Paper

1) Equations can LOOK tricky. They often use SYMBOLS to stand for different things.

2) But for all equations, all you have to do is
TIMES OR DIVIDE ONE NUMBER BY ANOTHER.

3) It's really useful to know equations off by heart.

4) But MOST of the equations you need will be on
an EQUATION SHEET in the exam paper. Hooray.

5) You just have to know WHICH EQUATION to use and HOW to use it.

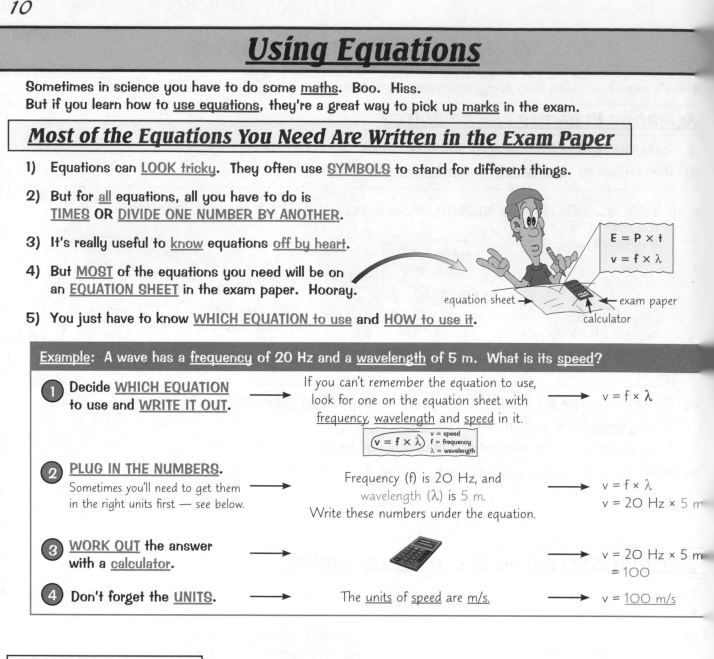

equation sheet →   ← exam paper
calculator

Example: A wave has a frequency of 20 Hz and a wavelength of 5 m. What is its speed?

1 Decide WHICH EQUATION to use and WRITE IT OUT. → If you can't remember the equation to use, look for one on the equation sheet with frequency, wavelength and speed in it. → $v = f \times \lambda$

$v = f \times \lambda$ v = speed f = frequency λ = wavelength

2 PLUG IN THE NUMBERS. Sometimes you'll need to get them in the right units first — see below. → Frequency (f) is 20 Hz, and wavelength (λ) is 5 m. Write these numbers under the equation. → $v = f \times \lambda$ $v = 20 \text{ Hz} \times 5 \text{ m}$

3 WORK OUT the answer with a calculator. → → $v = 20 \text{ Hz} \times 5 \text{ m}$ $= 100$

4 Don't forget the UNITS. → The units of speed are m/s. → $v = \underline{100 \text{ m/s}}$

Check Your Units

1) Before you plug the numbers in, check the numbers in the question have the RIGHT UNITS.

2) You need to LEARN what the RIGHT UNITS are for the things in the equations.

3) For example, wavelength ALWAYS needs to be in metres (m) to use the wave speed equation.

4) If you're given a wavelength in centimetres, you have to change it to metres BEFORE you use the equatio

Another Example: Find the energy, in kWh, transferred by a 1.5 kW hair drier in 30 minutes.

- Work out which equation you need to use: → $E = P \times t$ E = energy P = power t = time
- The power, P, is 1.5 kW. The time, t, is 30 minutes.
- But to get energy, E, in kWh (kilowatt-hours), the time needs to be in HOURS.
- There are 60 minutes in an hour. So 30 minutes = 30 ÷ 60 = 0.5 hours.
- Now you can plug the numbers into the equation: $E = P \times t$
  $E = 1.5 \text{ kW} \times 0.5 \text{ h}$
  $E = \underline{0.75 \text{ kWh}}$

5) Remember you always need to give the right units with your ANSWER too.

Diet and Metabolic Rate

The first page in this section is all about <u>food</u>. Yum.

A Good Diet Keeps You Healthy

1) Your <u>DIET</u> is what <u>food</u> you eat.

2) To be <u>HEALTHY</u> your <u>diet</u> must give you:
- The <u>ENERGY</u> you need.
- The right <u>AMOUNT</u> of <u>different foods</u>. This is called a <u>balanced diet</u>.

3) This means your <u>diet</u> must be made up of:

<u>FATS</u> — to keep you <u>warm</u> and give you <u>energy</u>.

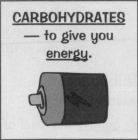

<u>CARBOHYDRATES</u> — to give you <u>energy</u>.

<u>VITAMINS</u> and <u>MINERALS</u> — to keep your <u>body healthy</u>.

<u>PROTEIN</u> — to <u>build cells</u> in your body.

Different People have Different Metabolic Rates

1) Your <u>METABOLISM</u> is all of the <u>chemical reactions</u> in the your body.

2) The <u>speed</u> these reactions happen at is called your <u>METABOLIC RATE</u>.

3) <u>Different people</u> have <u>different metabolic rates</u>:

① People with <u>lots of MUSCLE</u> have a <u>FAST</u> metabolic rate.

② People who do lots of <u>EXERCISE</u> have a <u>FAST</u> metabolic rate.

People with an <u>ACTIVE</u> job have a <u>FAST</u> metabolic rate.

③ The <u>GENES</u> you get from your <u>parents</u> can affect your metabolic rate.

Practice Questions

1) Which of these gives you <u>energy</u> — <u>vitamins</u> or <u>carbohydrates</u>?

2) What is <u>protein</u> needed for?

3) If you have an <u>active</u> job, will you have a <u>fast</u> or <u>slow</u> metabolic rate?

Being Healthy

Being <u>healthy</u> means having a <u>balanced diet</u> and not having any <u>diseases</u>.

An Unbalanced Diet is Bad for You

1) An <u>unbalanced diet</u> can be where people <u>eat too much</u>. Or it can be where people <u>eat too little</u>.

Eating <u>too much</u> can make a person
<u>OVERWEIGHT</u> or <u>OBESE</u> (very overweight).

Eating <u>too little</u> can make
a person <u>UNDERWEIGHT</u>.

2) People who eat an unbalanced diet are called <u>MALNOURISHED</u>.

3) Malnourished people can have <u>health problems</u>, for example:

- <u>TYPE 2 DIABETES</u> — this is where someone <u>can't control</u> the level of <u>sugar</u> in their <u>blood</u>.
- <u>DEFICIENCY DISEASES</u> — you get these from not eating enough <u>vitamins</u> or <u>minerals</u>.

Not Getting Enough Exercise is Also Bad for You

People who
<u>EXERCISE</u> a lot...

... are usually
<u>HEALTHIER</u> than
people who
don't exercise.

Your Genes can Affect Your Health

The <u>genes</u> you get from your parents can affect your:

1 METABOLIC RATE

1) Some people are born with a <u>SLOW</u> metabolic rate.
2) This can cause <u>OBESITY</u>.

2 CHOLESTEROL LEVEL

1) <u>Cholesterol</u> is a <u>type of fat</u> found in your body.
2) Some people have <u>TOO MUCH</u> cholesterol because of their genes.
3) This means they might get <u>HEART DISEASE</u>.

Practice Questions

1) Name <u>one health problem</u> that <u>malnourished people</u> can have.
2) "People who <u>exercise a lot</u> are usually <u>healthier</u> than people who don't exercise." True or false?
3) What might happen if someone has <u>too much cholesterol</u>?

Losing Weight

How can you tell if a <u>food</u> or <u>diet</u> will help you to <u>lose weight</u>... Well, read on to find out.

Diet and Exercise Can Help You Lose Weight

1) How much you <u>weigh</u> depends on how much <u>energy</u> you <u>TAKE IN</u> and how much <u>energy</u> you <u>USE</u>.

2) When you <u>EAT</u> you <u>take in</u> energy.

3) When you <u>EXERCISE</u> you <u>use</u> energy.

4) To <u>lose weight</u> you need to <u>TAKE IN LESS ENERGY THAN YOU USE</u>.

5) This means to <u>lose weight</u> you need to:

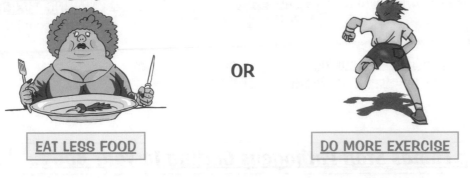

OR

EAT LESS FOOD   DO MORE EXERCISE

Some Foods Say They'll Help You Lose Weight

1) There are loads of <u>foods</u>, <u>drinks</u> and <u>diets</u> that say they'll help you <u>LOSE WEIGHT</u>. For example, slimming milkshakes.

2) But do they really work? You need to <u>look out</u> for <u>these things</u>:

- Is the report a PROPER SCIENTIFIC STUDY?
- Was it written by a PROPER SCIENTIST?
- Did the study ask LOTS of people?
- Have OTHER STUDIES found the same results?

<u>YES</u>

The claim could be <u>TRUE</u>.

<u>NO</u>

The claim may <u>NOT</u> be <u>TRUE</u>.

Practice Questions

1) Give <u>one</u> way a person can <u>take in less energy</u>.

2) Give <u>one</u> way a person can <u>use more energy</u>.

3) Slimming foods say they'll help you lose weight. Name <u>one</u> thing you need to look out for to see if it's <u>true</u>.

Fighting Disease

There are little nasties out there that can make you ill. But your body has some clever ways to protect you

Microorganisms Are Really, Really Tiny Organisms

1) Some microorganisms cause infectious diseases. They're called pathogens.

2) There are two main types of pathogen:

Infectious disease are diseases that can be caught.

1. BACTERIA

1) Bacteria reproduce (copy themselves) very quickly inside your body.

2) They make you feel ill by: (1) DAMAGING YOUR CELLS   (2) MAKING TOXINS (poisons)

2. VIRUSES

1) Viruses reproduce very quickly inside your cells.

2) Viruses make you feel ill by DAMAGING YOUR CELLS.

These Three Things Stop Pathogens Getting In Your Body...

1) HAIRS and MUCUS in your nose.

2) SKIN

3) SCABS (If you cut your skin, your blood clots and makes a scab.)

The Immune System Kills Pathogens

1) The main bit of the immune system is the WHITE BLOOD CELLS.

2) They do three things:

1. INGEST Pathogens

They take in pathogens and digest them.

white blood cell   pathogen

2. Make ANTIBODIES

pathogen   antibody

(1) When a pathogen comes along...   (2) ... white blood cells make antibodies.   (3) Antibodies kill the microorganism.

3. Make ANTITOXINS   These STOP TOXINS made by bacteria.

Practice Questions

1) How do viruses make you feel ill?

2) Name one thing that stops pathogens getting inside your body.

3) What are the three things that white blood cells do?

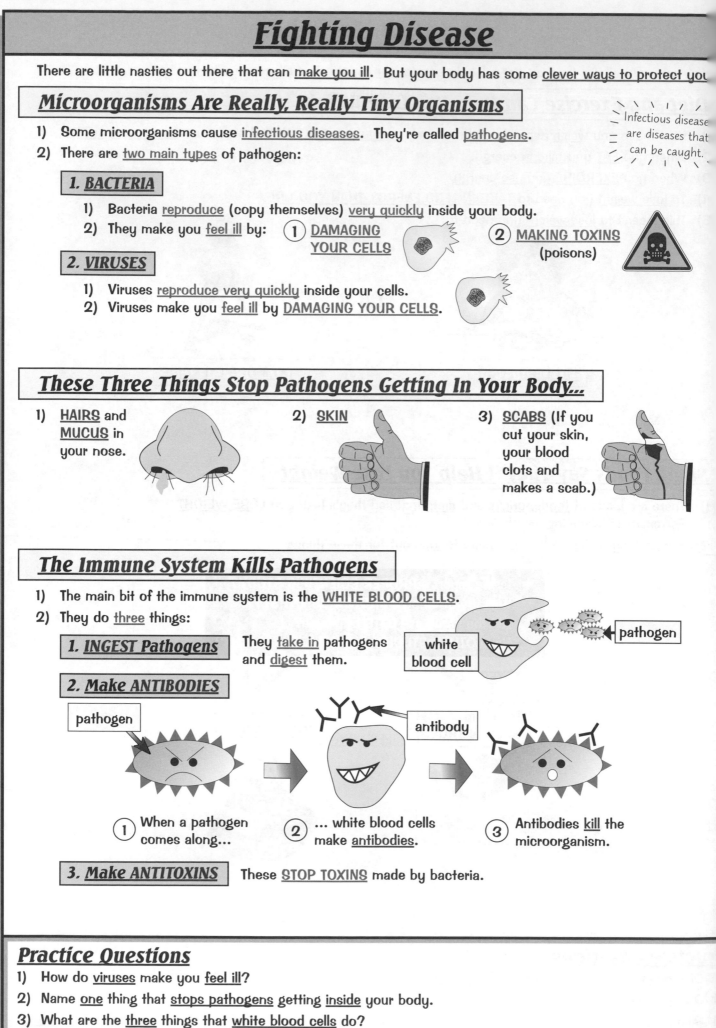

Vaccines

Some diseases are so horrible you really <u>don't want</u> to get them. But <u>don't worry</u> — you can help your body <u>fight</u> the little nasties that cause them. You do this by having a <u>vaccine</u>. Oh what fun...

A Vaccine is an Injection of Dead or Inactive Pathogens

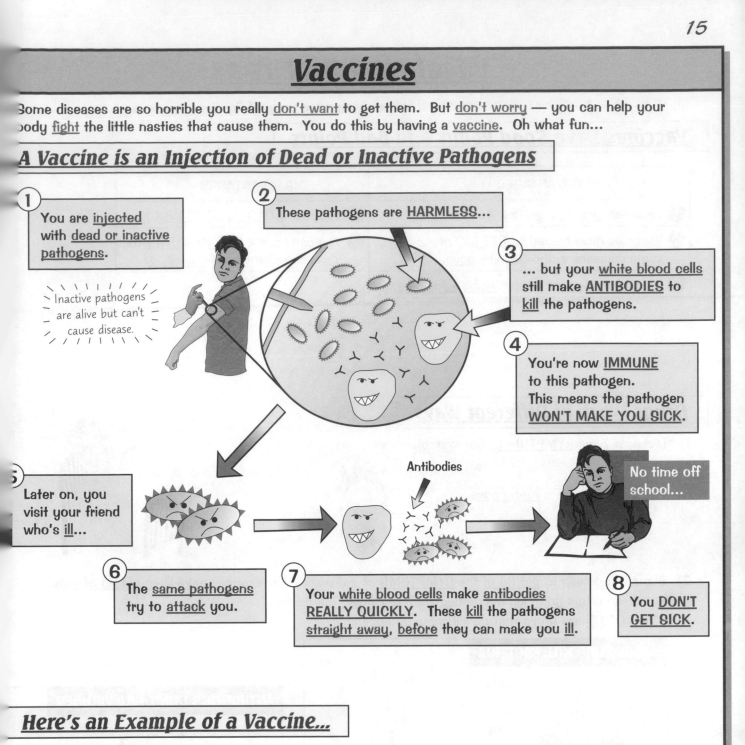

1 You are <u>injected</u> with <u>dead or inactive pathogens</u>.

~ Inactive pathogens are alive but can't cause disease.

2 These pathogens are <u>HARMLESS</u>...

3 ... but your <u>white blood cells</u> still make <u>ANTIBODIES</u> to <u>kill</u> the pathogens.

4 You're now <u>IMMUNE</u> to this pathogen. This means the pathogen <u>WON'T MAKE YOU SICK</u>.

5 Later on, you visit your friend who's <u>ill</u>...

Antibodies

No time off school...

6 The <u>same pathogens</u> try to <u>attack</u> you.

7 Your <u>white blood cells</u> make <u>antibodies</u> <u>REALLY QUICKLY</u>. These <u>kill</u> the pathogens <u>straight away</u>, <u>before</u> they can make you <u>ill</u>.

8 You <u>DON'T GET SICK</u>.

Here's an Example of a Vaccine...

1) The <u>MMR vaccine</u> is given to <u>children</u>.
2) It <u>protects</u> them from three diseases — <u>MEASLES</u>, <u>MUMPS</u> and <u>RUBELLA</u>.

Vaccines Won't Work Against New Viruses

1) Viruses can <u>mutate</u> (change) to make <u>new viruses</u>.
2) This can lead to <u>VACCINES NOT WORKING</u> any more.
3) A new virus could <u>spread all over the world</u> — this is called a <u>PANDEMIC</u>.

Practice Questions

1) "Vaccines use pathogens that are <u>harmless</u>." True or false?
2) What does it means if you're <u>immune</u> to a pathogen?
3) Which <u>three diseases</u> does the <u>MMR</u> vaccine protect you from?

Vaccines and Drugs

Uh oh — as well as vaccines, it looks like there are <u>even more ways</u> of fighting disease...

Vaccines have Good Points and Bad Points

ADVANTAGES 👍	DISADVANTAGES 👎
❶ Vaccines <u>stop you getting ill</u>.	❶ Vaccines <u>DON'T ALWAYS WORK</u>.
❷ Vaccines have helped to <u>GET RID</u> of some diseases in the UK, like <u>polio</u>.	❷ You can have a <u>BAD REACTION</u> to a vaccine, for example <u>swelling</u>.
❸ Vaccinating <u>lots</u> of people <u>stops epidemics</u>.	

An <u>EPIDEMIC</u> is a <u>big outbreak</u> of a disease.

Drugs Work in Different Ways

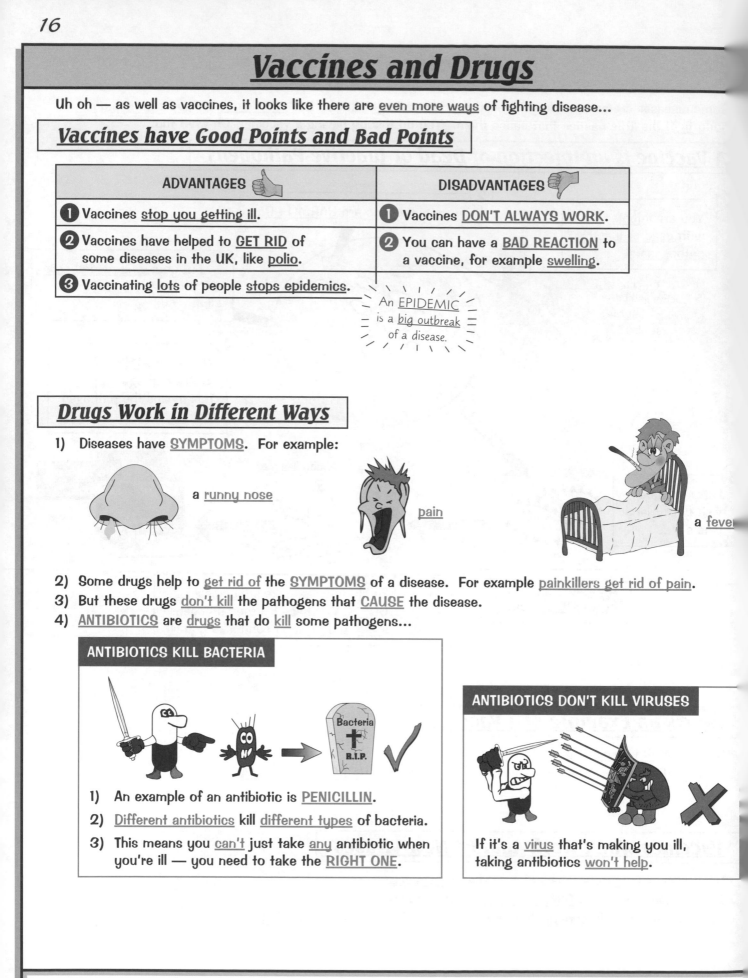

1) Diseases have <u>SYMPTOMS</u>. For example:

a <u>runny nose</u>

<u>pain</u>

a <u>fever</u>

2) Some drugs help to <u>get rid of</u> the <u>SYMPTOMS</u> of a disease. For example <u>painkillers get rid of pain</u>.

3) But these drugs <u>don't kill</u> the pathogens that <u>CAUSE</u> the disease.

4) <u>ANTIBIOTICS</u> are <u>drugs</u> that do <u>kill</u> some pathogens...

ANTIBIOTICS KILL BACTERIA

Bacteria R.I.P.

1) An example of an antibiotic is <u>PENICILLIN</u>.

2) <u>Different antibiotics</u> kill <u>different types</u> of bacteria.

3) This means you <u>can't</u> just take <u>any</u> antibiotic when you're ill — you need to take the <u>RIGHT ONE</u>.

ANTIBIOTICS DON'T KILL VIRUSES

If it's a <u>virus</u> that's making you ill, taking antibiotics <u>won't help</u>.

Practice Questions

1) Give <u>one advantage</u> of vaccines.

2) What <u>type</u> of <u>pathogen</u> do antibiotics kill?

3) Why do you need to get the <u>right antibiotic</u> when you're ill?

Antibiotic Resistance

Antibiotics are great — but they do have their problems...

Bacteria Can Become Resistant to Antibiotics

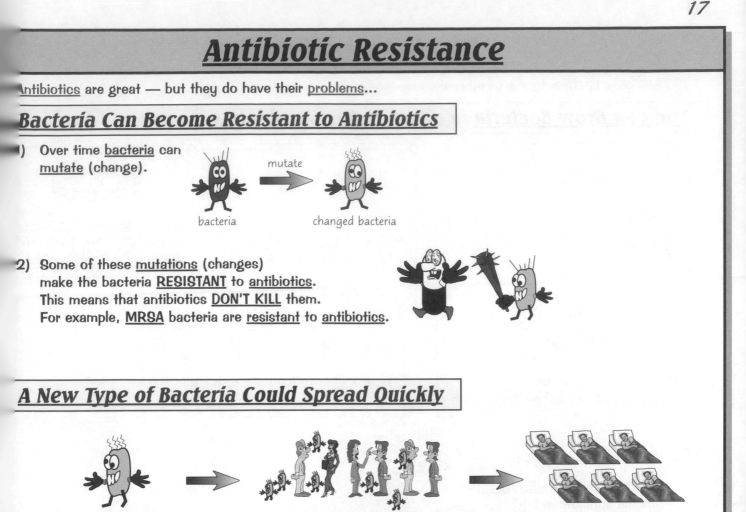

1) Over time bacteria can mutate (change).

bacteria   changed bacteria

2) Some of these mutations (changes) make the bacteria RESISTANT to antibiotics. This means that antibiotics DON'T KILL them. For example, MRSA bacteria are resistant to antibiotics.

A New Type of Bacteria Could Spread Quickly

1) Bacteria could mutate to produce a new type that no-one is immune to.

2) This bacteria could spread quickly between people.

3) It could even cause an EPIDEMIC — a big outbreak of disease.

More Bacteria are Now Resistant to Antibiotics

1) Today not many people die from diseases caused by bacteria.

2) This is because we have antibiotics to kill the bacteria.

3) BUT... MORE AND MORE bacteria are now resistant to antibiotics.

4) You can make it HARDER for bacteria to become resistant to antibiotics. You can do this by ONLY using antibiotics when you really need to. For example, for serious infections and not for things like sore throats.

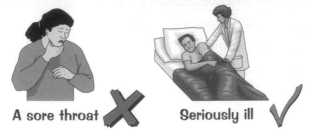

A sore throat ✗   Seriously ill ✓

Practice Questions

1) What does it mean if bacteria are resistant to antibiotics?

2) Give one example of bacteria that are resistant to antibiotics.

3) What is an epidemic?

Testing Antibiotics

You can grow bacteria to see whether they are <u>resistant</u> to an antibiotic or not...

You Can Grow Bacteria in a Dish to Test Antibiotics

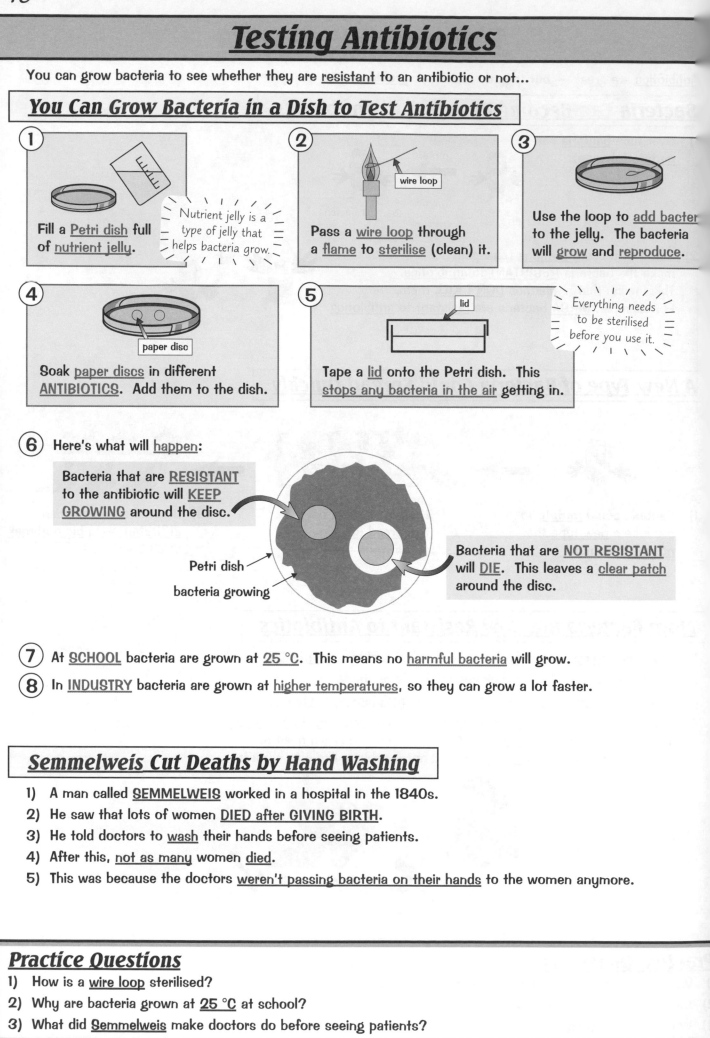

(1) Fill a <u>Petri dish</u> full of <u>nutrient jelly</u>.

Nutrient jelly is a type of jelly that helps bacteria grow.

(2) Pass a <u>wire loop</u> through a <u>flame</u> to <u>sterilise</u> (clean) it.

wire loop

(3) Use the loop to <u>add bacter</u> to the jelly. The bacteria will <u>grow</u> and <u>reproduce</u>.

(4) Soak <u>paper discs</u> in different <u>ANTIBIOTICS</u>. Add them to the dish.

paper disc

(5) Tape a <u>lid</u> onto the Petri dish. This <u>stops any bacteria in the air</u> getting in.

lid

Everything needs to be sterilised before you use it.

(6) Here's what will <u>happen</u>:

Bacteria that are <u>RESISTANT</u> to the antibiotic will <u>KEEP GROWING</u> around the disc.

Petri dish

bacteria growing

Bacteria that are <u>NOT RESISTANT</u> will <u>DIE</u>. This leaves a <u>clear patch</u> around the disc.

(7) At <u>SCHOOL</u> bacteria are grown at <u>25 °C</u>. This means no <u>harmful bacteria</u> will grow.

(8) In <u>INDUSTRY</u> bacteria are grown at <u>higher temperatures</u>, so they can grow a lot faster.

Semmelweis Cut Deaths by Hand Washing

1) A man called <u>SEMMELWEIS</u> worked in a hospital in the 1840s.
2) He saw that lots of women <u>DIED after GIVING BIRTH</u>.
3) He told doctors to <u>wash</u> their hands before seeing patients.
4) After this, <u>not as many</u> women <u>died</u>.
5) This was because the doctors <u>weren't passing bacteria on their hands</u> to the women anymore.

Practice Questions

1) How is a <u>wire loop</u> sterilised?
2) Why are bacteria grown at <u>25 °C</u> at school?
3) What did <u>Semmelweis</u> make doctors do before seeing patients?

Biology 1a — Human Biology

The Nervous System

The nervous system allows you to react to what goes on around you — life would be tough without it.

Sense Organs Detect Stimuli

1) You have five different SENSE ORGANS — EYES, EARS, NOSE, TONGUE and SKIN.

2) They all have different RECEPTORS in them.

3) Receptors are groups of cells that DETECT A STIMULUS.

4) A STIMULUS is a CHANGE in your environment which you may need to react to.
For example, a lion charging at you.

5) Here are the five sense organs and the stimuli they detect...

Stimuli are changes in your environment.

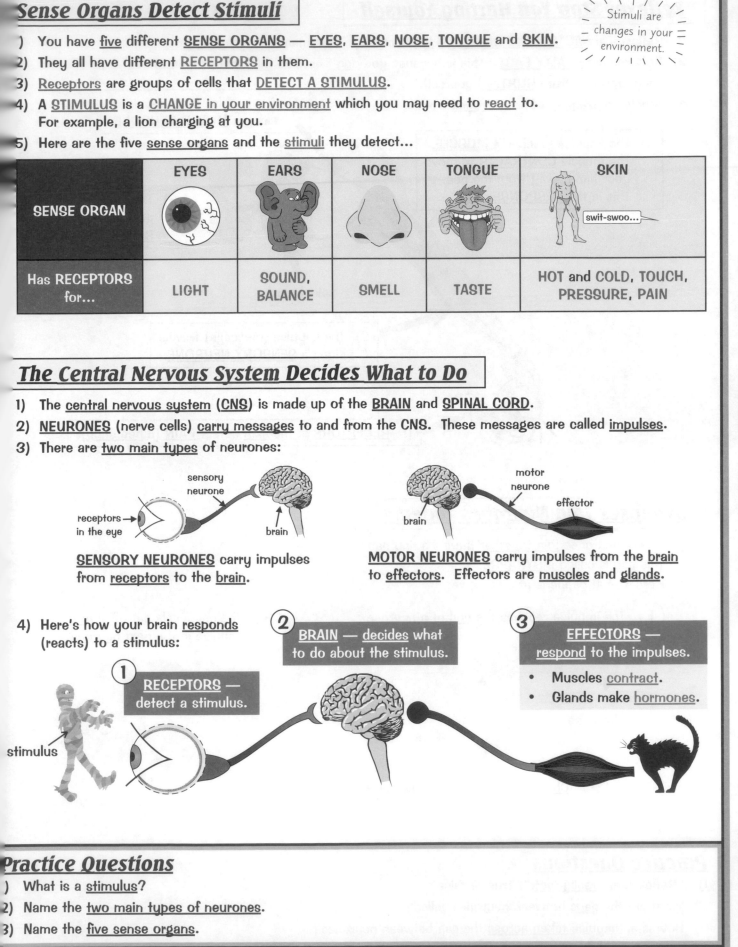

SENSE ORGAN	EYES	EARS	NOSE	TONGUE	SKIN
Has RECEPTORS for...	LIGHT	SOUND, BALANCE	SMELL	TASTE	HOT and COLD, TOUCH, PRESSURE, PAIN

swit-swoo...

The Central Nervous System Decides What to Do

1) The central nervous system (CNS) is made up of the BRAIN and SPINAL CORD.

2) NEURONES (nerve cells) carry messages to and from the CNS. These messages are called impulses.

3) There are two main types of neurones:

receptors → in the eye
sensory neurone
brain

SENSORY NEURONES carry impulses from receptors to the brain.

brain
motor neurone
effector

MOTOR NEURONES carry impulses from the brain to effectors. Effectors are muscles and glands.

4) Here's how your brain responds (reacts) to a stimulus:

① RECEPTORS — detect a stimulus.

② BRAIN — decides what to do about the stimulus.

③ EFFECTORS — respond to the impulses.
• Muscles contract.
• Glands make hormones.

stimulus

Practice Questions

1) What is a stimulus?

2) Name the two main types of neurones.

3) Name the five sense organs.

Reflexes and Synapses

Messages can be sent really, really fast. Useful — you can avoid that football coming straight at your face

Reflexes Stop You Hurting Yourself

1) Reflexes are AUTOMATIC RESPONSES (reactions). This means they just happen.
2) Reflexes are REALLY FAST. This is because you don't have to think about them.
3) They stop you from HURTING yourself.
4) Here's an example of how a reflex works:

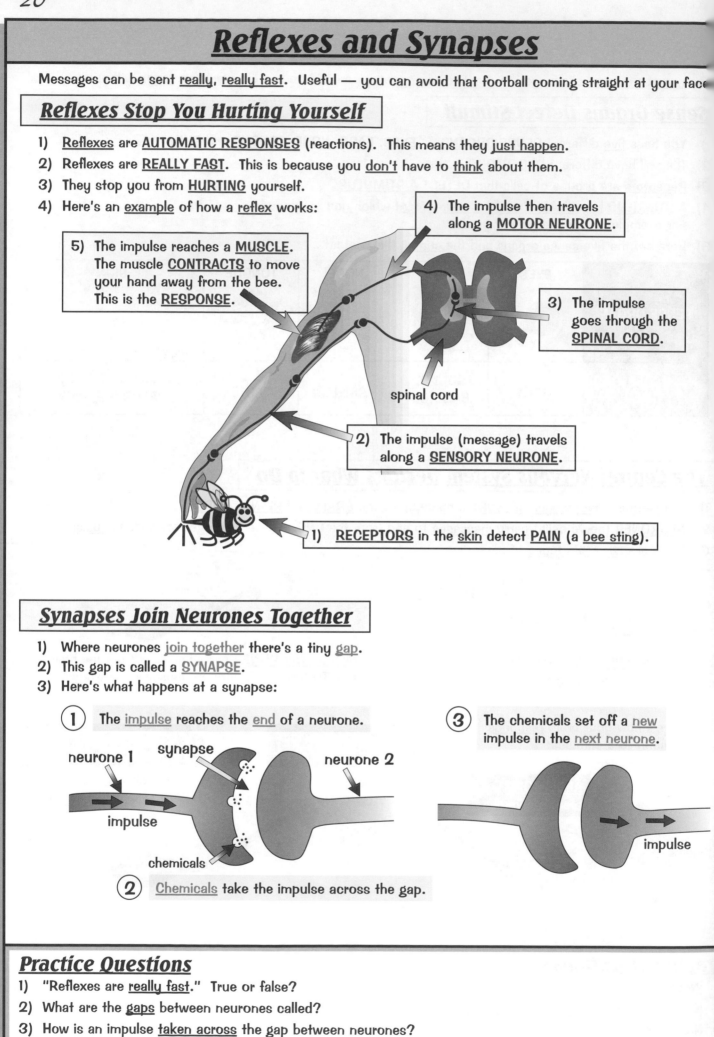

5) The impulse reaches a MUSCLE. The muscle CONTRACTS to move your hand away from the bee. This is the RESPONSE.

4) The impulse then travels along a MOTOR NEURONE.

3) The impulse goes through the SPINAL CORD.

spinal cord

2) The impulse (message) travels along a SENSORY NEURONE.

1) RECEPTORS in the skin detect PAIN (a bee sting).

Synapses Join Neurones Together

1) Where neurones join together there's a tiny gap.
2) This gap is called a SYNAPSE.
3) Here's what happens at a synapse:

① The impulse reaches the end of a neurone.

③ The chemicals set off a new impulse in the next neurone.

neurone 1
synapse
neurone 2

impulse

chemicals

② Chemicals take the impulse across the gap.

impulse

Practice Questions

1) "Reflexes are really fast." True or false?
2) What are the gaps between neurones called?
3) How is an impulse taken across the gap between neurones?

Hormones and The Menstrual Cycle

Messages go around the body using <u>nerves</u> or <u>hormones</u>. This page is all about <u>hormones</u>.

Hormones Are Chemicals Sent in the Blood

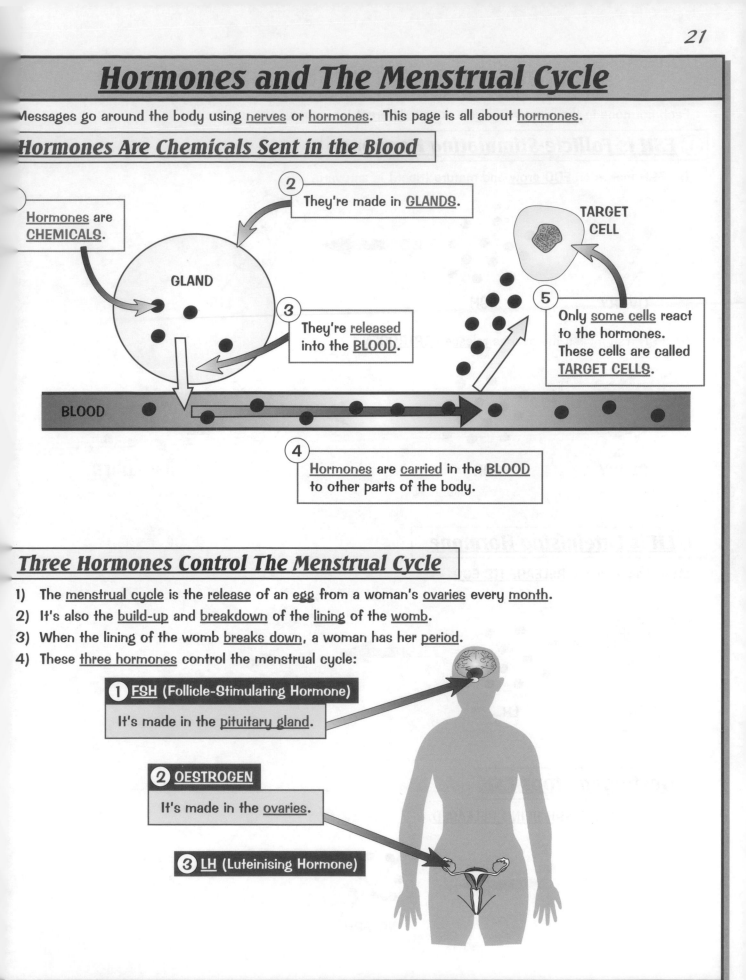

Hormones are <u>CHEMICALS</u>.

2 They're made in <u>GLANDS</u>.

GLAND

3 They're <u>released</u> into the <u>BLOOD</u>.

TARGET CELL

5 Only <u>some cells</u> react to the hormones. These cells are called <u>TARGET CELLS</u>.

BLOOD

4 <u>Hormones</u> are <u>carried</u> in the <u>BLOOD</u> to other parts of the body.

Three Hormones Control The Menstrual Cycle

1) The <u>menstrual cycle</u> is the <u>release</u> of an <u>egg</u> from a woman's <u>ovaries</u> every <u>month</u>.

2) It's also the <u>build-up</u> and <u>breakdown</u> of the <u>lining</u> of the <u>womb</u>.

3) When the lining of the womb <u>breaks down</u>, a woman has her <u>period</u>.

4) These <u>three hormones</u> control the menstrual cycle:

1 <u>FSH</u> (Follicle-Stimulating Hormone)

It's made in the <u>pituitary gland</u>.

2 <u>OESTROGEN</u>

It's made in the <u>ovaries</u>.

3 <u>LH</u> (Luteinising Hormone)

Practice Questions

1) What are <u>hormones</u>?

2) What are the <u>cells</u> that react to hormones called?

3) Name <u>three hormones</u> that control the <u>menstrual cycle</u>.

Biology 1a — Human Biology

Hormones and The Menstrual Cycle

Each hormone in the menstrual cycle does a <u>different job</u>...

① *FSH is Follicle-Stimulating Hormone*

1) FSH makes an <u>EGG grow</u> and <u>mature</u> (ripen) in an ovary.

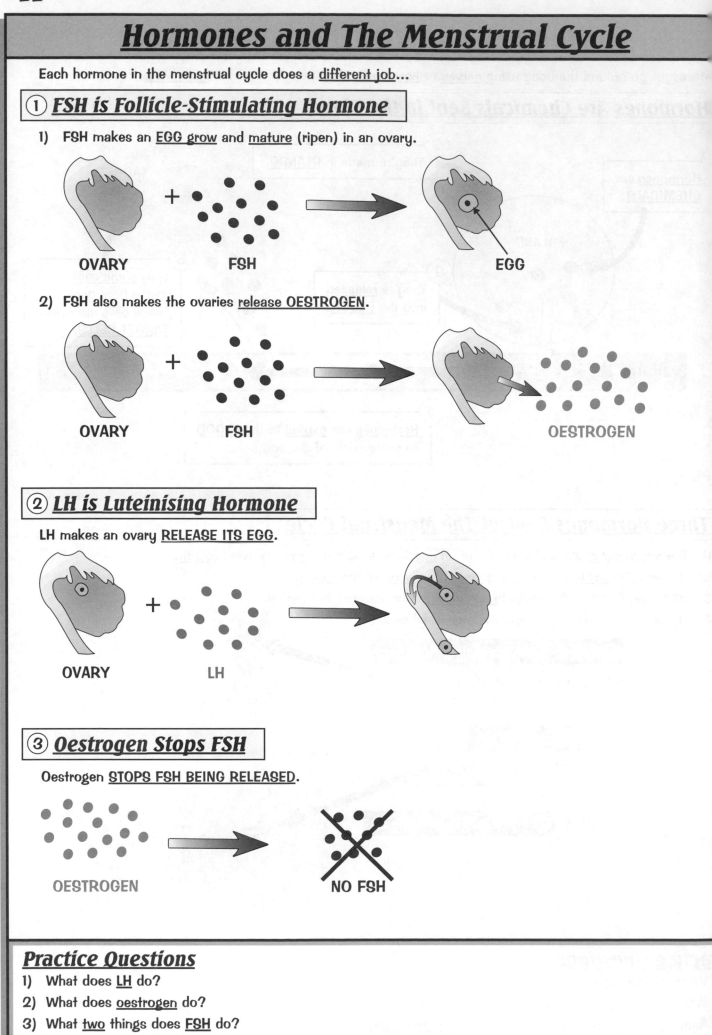

OVARY + **FSH** → **EGG**

2) FSH also makes the ovaries <u>release OESTROGEN</u>.

OVARY + **FSH** → **OESTROGEN**

② *LH is Luteinising Hormone*

LH makes an ovary <u>RELEASE ITS EGG</u>.

OVARY + **LH** →

③ *Oestrogen Stops FSH*

Oestrogen <u>STOPS FSH BEING RELEASED</u>.

OESTROGEN → **NO FSH**

Practice Questions

1) What does <u>LH</u> do?
2) What does <u>oestrogen</u> do?
3) What <u>two</u> things does <u>FSH</u> do?

The Pill

Hormones can be used to <u>change</u> how <u>fertile</u> a woman is (how able she is to have children).

The Pill Can Stop a Woman Getting Pregnant

The pill is a <u>tablet</u> women take to <u>stop them getting pregnant</u>. It's called an <u>oral contraceptive</u>.

oestrogen
progesterone

FSH

A woman takes the <u>pill</u>.
It has <u>OESTROGEN</u> and
<u>PROGESTERONE</u> in it.

Oestrogen <u>stops FSH</u>
being released.

<u>NO EGGS</u> mature.

This means the woman
<u>can't</u> get <u>pregnant</u>.

*Progesterone is another hormone.
It can also stop you getting pregnant.*

The Pill has Advantages and Disadvantages...

ADVANTAGES 👍	DISADVANTAGES 👎
❶ Women <u>don't usually</u> get <u>pregnant</u>.	❶ There's still a <u>very small chance</u> of getting pregnant.
❷ Women are <u>less likely</u> to get some <u>cancers</u>.	❷ It can cause <u>side effects</u>, for example <u>headaches</u>.

The Pill has Less Oestrogen In It Than it Used To

① <u>The pill</u> used to have
<u>A LOT</u> of <u>oestrogen</u> in.

But people worried that
this caused <u>SIDE EFFECTS</u>.

② <u>The pill</u> now has <u>LESS</u> oestrogen in.

This means there <u>aren't</u>
as many <u>side effects</u>.

③ There's also a tablet called
the <u>progesterone-only pill</u>.
It <u>only</u> has <u>progesterone</u> in it.

The <u>progesterone-only pill</u>
has <u>fewer side effects</u> than
the pill.

Practice Questions

1) The pill has <u>two hormones</u> in it. What are these hormones called?
2) Give <u>one advantage</u> of the pill.
3) Give <u>one disadvantage</u> of the pill.

Getting Pregnant

Hormones can also be used to <u>help</u> a woman to have a <u>baby</u>.

FSH and LH Can Help a Woman to Get Pregnant

Some <u>hormones</u> can be taken to <u>help</u> a woman get pregnant:

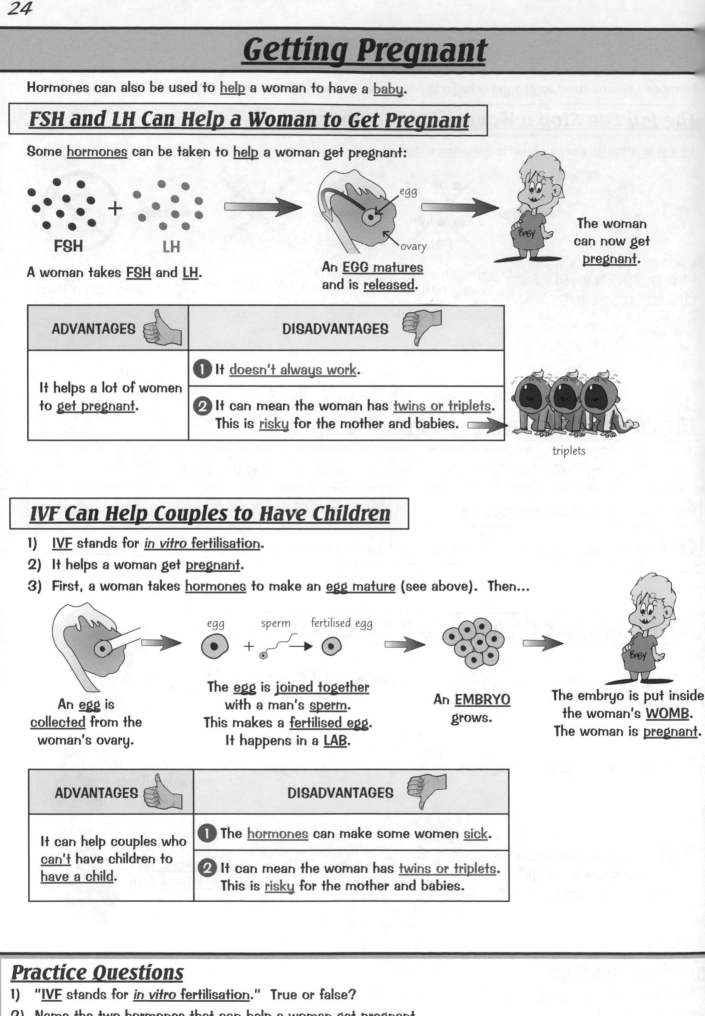

A woman takes <u>FSH</u> and <u>LH</u>.

An <u>EGG</u> matures and is <u>released</u>.

The woman can now get <u>pregnant</u>.

ADVANTAGES	DISADVANTAGES
It helps a lot of women to <u>get pregnant</u>.	❶ It <u>doesn't always work</u>. ❷ It can mean the woman has <u>twins or triplets</u>. This is <u>risky</u> for the mother and babies.

triplets

IVF Can Help Couples to Have Children

1) <u>IVF</u> stands for *in vitro* fertilisation.
2) It helps a woman get <u>pregnant</u>.
3) First, a woman takes <u>hormones</u> to make an <u>egg mature</u> (see above). Then...

egg   sperm   fertilised egg

An <u>egg</u> is <u>collected</u> from the woman's ovary.

The <u>egg</u> is <u>joined together</u> with a man's <u>sperm</u>. This makes a <u>fertilised egg</u>. It happens in a <u>LAB</u>.

An <u>EMBRYO</u> grows.

The embryo is put inside the woman's <u>WOMB</u>. The woman is <u>pregnant</u>.

ADVANTAGES	DISADVANTAGES
It can help couples who <u>can't</u> have children to <u>have a child</u>.	❶ The <u>hormones</u> can make some women <u>sick</u>. ❷ It can mean the woman has <u>twins or triplets</u>. This is <u>risky</u> for the mother and babies.

Practice Questions

1) "<u>IVF</u> stands for *in vitro* fertilisation." True or false?
2) Name the <u>two hormones</u> that can help a woman get pregnant.
3) Give <u>one disadvantage</u> of IVF.

Plant Hormones

If you're wondering what <u>plants</u> are doing in this section... well, they have <u>hormones</u> too, you know.

Auxin is a Plant Growth Hormone

1) <u>Plant growth</u> is controlled by <u>hormones</u>.

2) <u>AUXIN</u> is a <u>hormone</u> that controls <u>plant growth</u>.

3) Auxin does different things:

> ① Auxin makes plants grow in response to <u>light</u>. This is called <u>PHOTOTROPISM</u>.

> ② Auxin makes plants grow in response to <u>gravity</u>. This is called <u>GRAVITROPISM</u>.

> ③ Auxin also makes plants grow in response to <u>moisture</u>.

Auxin Makes Shoots Grow Towards Light

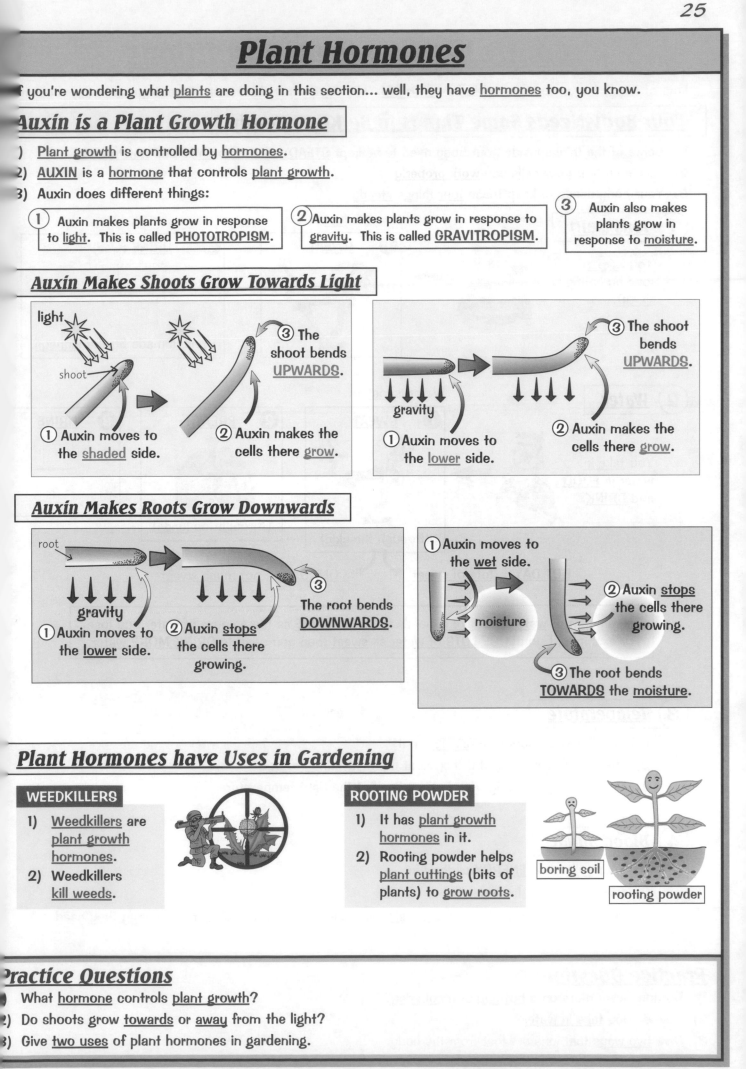

light
shoot
③ The shoot bends <u>UPWARDS</u>.
① Auxin moves to the <u>shaded</u> side.
② Auxin makes the cells there <u>grow</u>.

③ The shoot bends <u>UPWARDS</u>.
gravity
① Auxin moves to the <u>lower</u> side.
② Auxin makes the cells there <u>grow</u>.

Auxin Makes Roots Grow Downwards

root
gravity
① Auxin moves to the <u>lower</u> side.
② Auxin <u>stops</u> the cells there growing.
③ The root bends <u>DOWNWARDS</u>.

① Auxin moves to the <u>wet</u> side.
moisture
② Auxin <u>stops</u> the cells there growing.
③ The root bends <u>TOWARDS</u> the <u>moisture</u>.

Plant Hormones have Uses in Gardening

WEEDKILLERS

1) <u>Weedkillers</u> are <u>plant growth hormones</u>.

2) <u>Weedkillers</u> <u>kill weeds</u>.

ROOTING POWDER

1) It has <u>plant growth hormones</u> in it.

2) Rooting powder helps <u>plant cuttings</u> (bits of plants) to <u>grow roots</u>.

boring soil
rooting powder

Practice Questions

1) What <u>hormone</u> controls <u>plant growth</u>?

2) Do shoots grow <u>towards</u> or <u>away</u> from the light?

3) Give <u>two uses</u> of plant hormones in gardening.

Biology 1a — Human Biology

Controlling Internal Conditions

Lots of things in your body need to be <u>controlled</u>. Luckily, your body does it without you thinking about it.

Your Body Needs Some Things to Be Kept Steady

1) Some of the things inside your body need to be kept <u>STEADY</u> — <u>not too high</u> and <u>not too low</u>.

2) This is so that your <u>cells</u> can <u>work properly</u>.

3) Your body needs to keep these <u>four</u> things <u>steady</u>:

① **Ions (salt)**

You <u>take in</u> ions by eating <u>FOOD</u>.

Ions are <u>lost</u> in:

① **SWEAT**

② **URINE** (wee)

Urine is made by the <u>kidneys</u>.

② **Water**

You <u>take in</u> water in <u>FOOD</u> and <u>DRINK</u>.

Water is <u>lost</u> in:

① **SWEAT**

(through the <u>skin</u>)

② **BREATH**

(through the <u>lungs</u>)

③ **URINE**

<u>HOT DAY</u> = <u>lots of sweat</u>   <u>COLD DAY</u> = <u>not much sweat</u>

The amount of <u>water</u> you <u>take in</u> needs to be the <u>SAME</u> as the amount of <u>water</u> you <u>lose</u>. For example, if you <u>LOSE LOTS</u> of water as <u>sweat</u> then you need to <u>DRINK MORE</u> water.

③ **Temperature**

Enzymes speed up the chemical reactions in your body.

1) Your body has lots of <u>ENZYMES</u> in it.

2) The enzymes <u>work best</u> if they're at the <u>right temperature</u>.

3) This means your body tries to <u>keep itself</u> at the right temperature.

④ **Blood Sugar**

1) Your <u>cells</u> need <u>ENERGY</u> all the time.

2) Cells get energy from <u>sugar</u>.

3) Your body keeps the level of sugar <u>steady</u>. This means your cells get the energy they need.

Practice Questions

1) Do you sweat more on a <u>hot day</u> or a <u>cold day</u>?

2) How do you <u>take in water</u>?

3) Give <u>two ways</u> that ions are lost from the body.

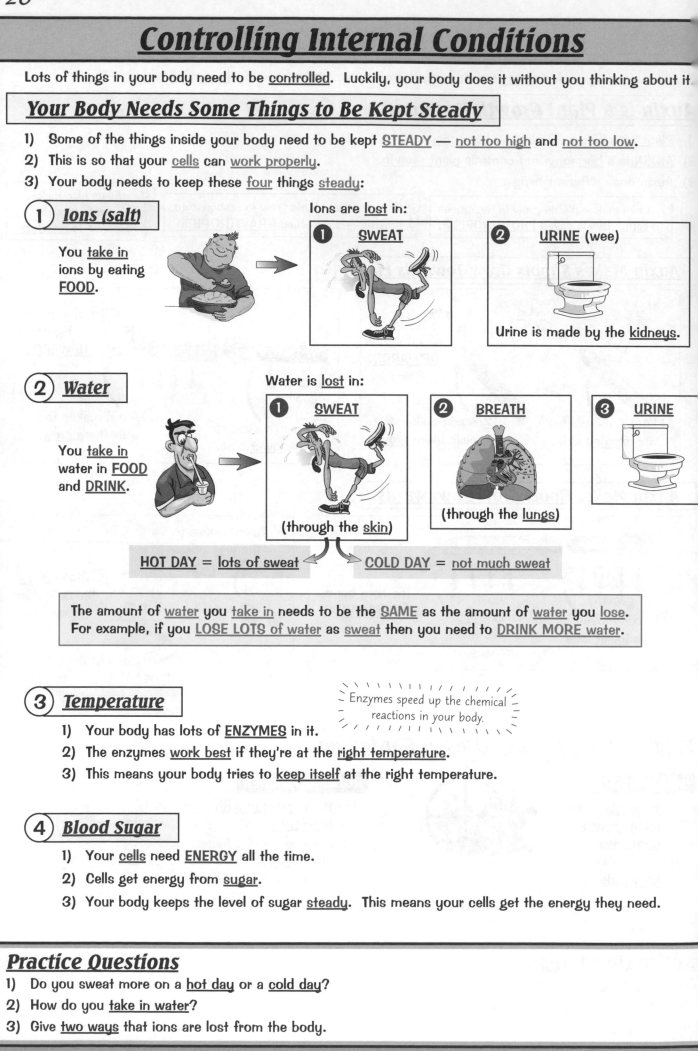

Drugs

Drugs change what's going on inside your body — sometimes for the better, sometimes not.

Drugs Change Your Body Chemistry

Must have drugs...

1) A <u>drug</u> changes the <u>chemical reactions</u> in your body.

2) Some people get <u>addicted</u> to drugs (want them really badly). <u>Heroin</u> and <u>cocaine</u> are <u>very addictive</u> drugs.

3) If the drug <u>isn't</u> taken they can get <u>withdrawal symptoms</u>. For example, they're <u>sick</u>.

Statins are a Medicine

1) Some drugs are <u>medicines</u>. For example, <u>statins</u>.
2) Statins are used to lower the risk of <u>heart</u> and <u>circulatory disease</u>.
3) If you need statins, your <u>doctor</u> will give you a <u>prescription</u> (note) for them.

Circulatory diseases are diseases of the heart and the blood vessels.

Performance-Enhancing Drugs make you Better at Sport

1) A <u>performance-enhancing</u> drug is a drug that makes athletes <u>better at sport</u>. For example, STEROIDS and STIMULANTS are performance-enhancing drugs.

(1) <u>Steroids</u> make your <u>muscles bigger</u>.

(2) <u>Stimulants</u> make your <u>heart rate faster</u>.

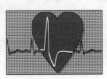

2) But these drugs can have <u>bad health effects</u>. For example, steroids can cause <u>high blood pressure</u>.

3) <u>Not all</u> performance-enhancing drugs are <u>allowed</u>:

(1)
Some of them are <u>illegal</u>.

(2)
Others are <u>legal</u> but you need to have a <u>prescription</u>.

(3)
<u>ALL</u> of them are <u>banned</u> in <u>sport</u>.

4) Here are some reasons <u>for</u> and <u>against</u> taking performance-enhancing drugs:

AGAINST ✗	FOR ✓
① It's <u>not fair</u> if people are better at sport <u>just</u> because they take drugs.	① Sport <u>isn't really fair</u> anyway, for example athletes may have <u>different coaches</u>.
② Athletes may <u>not know</u> about the <u>bad health effects</u>.	② Athletes can make their <u>own decision</u> about the health effects.

Practice Questions

1) What are <u>statins</u> used for?
2) Name <u>one</u> performance-enhancing drug.

Testing Medicines

Medicines are a really important type of drug.

New Drugs are Tested in Stages

1) Scientists are always making new drugs. These drugs are used as medicines.

2) Every drug that's used as a medicine has to be TESTED first.

3) There are three main stages in drug testing:

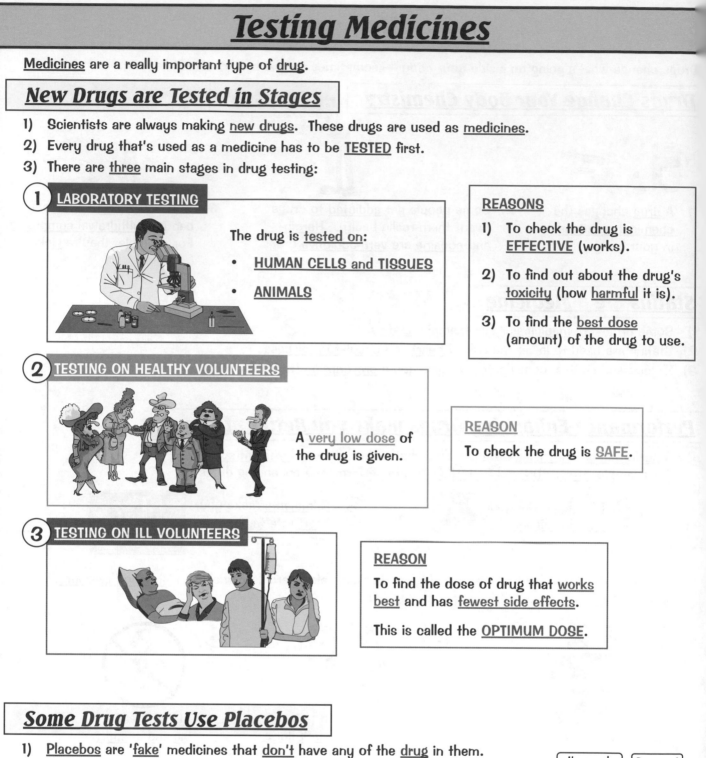

1 LABORATORY TESTING

The drug is tested on:

- HUMAN CELLS and TISSUES

- ANIMALS

REASONS

1) To check the drug is EFFECTIVE (works).

2) To find out about the drug's toxicity (how harmful it is).

3) To find the best dose (amount) of the drug to use.

2 TESTING ON HEALTHY VOLUNTEERS

A very low dose of the drug is given.

REASON

To check the drug is SAFE.

3 TESTING ON ILL VOLUNTEERS

REASON

To find the dose of drug that works best and has fewest side effects.

This is called the OPTIMUM DOSE.

Some Drug Tests Use Placebos

1) Placebos are 'fake' medicines that don't have any of the drug in them. This means that they DON'T DO ANYTHING.

2) They're given to some patients in a drug trial (test).

3) This checks it's the NEW DRUG that's making people better. (Some people can feel better if they're given something and told it'll help them.)

4) Sometimes the doctor and the patients DON'T KNOW which patients have taken the drug and which have taken the placebo. This is called a double-blind trial.

Practice Questions

1) "Placebos are real medicines with lots of the drug in them." True or false?

2) Name the first stage of drug testing.

3) Why is a drug tested on healthy volunteers?

Biology 1a — Human Biology

Thalidomide

f drugs aren't tested properly, things can go <u>wrong</u> ...

Thalidomide is a Drug that Wasn't Tested Properly

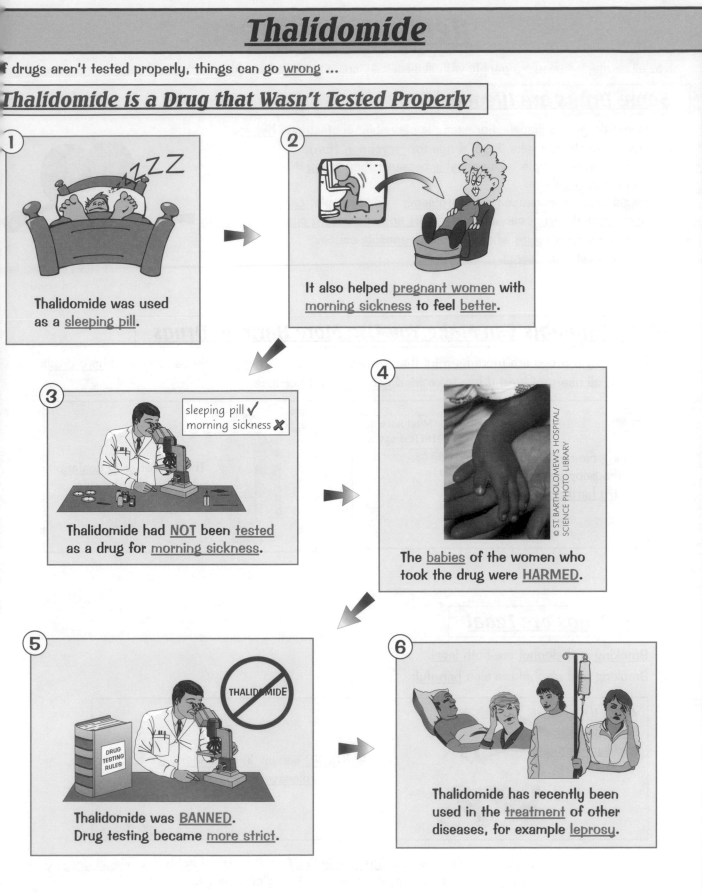

1 Thalidomide was used as a <u>sleeping pill</u>.

2 It also helped <u>pregnant women</u> with <u>morning sickness</u> to feel <u>better</u>.

3 sleeping pill ✓
morning sickness ✗

Thalidomide had <u>**NOT**</u> been <u>tested</u> as a drug for <u>morning sickness</u>.

4 © ST. BARTHOLOMEW'S HOSPITAL/ SCIENCE PHOTO LIBRARY

The <u>babies</u> of the women who took the drug were <u>HARMED</u>.

5 THALIDOMIDE

DRUG TESTING RULES

Thalidomide was <u>BANNED</u>. Drug testing became <u>more strict</u>.

6 Thalidomide has recently been used in the <u>treatment</u> of other diseases, for example <u>leprosy</u>.

Practice Questions

) What was <u>thalidomide</u> first used as?

) Had thalidomide been <u>tested</u> for <u>morning sickness</u>?

) "Thalidomide <u>has not</u> recently been used in the <u>treatment</u> of <u>other diseases</u>." True or false?

Recreational Drugs

Not all drugs are used by people with illnesses — some are used for <u>fun</u>.

Some Drugs are Illegal

1) Some drugs are <u>illegal</u>. For example <u>cannabis</u>, <u>ecstasy</u> and <u>heroin</u>.
2) Some people still take illegal drugs for <u>recreation</u> (fun). For example, people take <u>cannabis</u> because they <u>enjoy</u> it and it <u>relaxes</u> them.
3) Illegal drugs can cause <u>health problems</u>. For example, <u>cannabis</u>, <u>ecstasy</u> and <u>heroin</u> can all cause <u>heart and circulatory system problems</u>.
4) Scientists <u>aren't sure</u> whether or not <u>cannabis</u> causes <u>mental health problems</u>.

Your circulatory system includes your blood vessels.

Using Cannabis Can Make You Use More Harmful Drugs

1) Some illegal drugs are more <u>harmful</u> than others, for example <u>heroin</u>. These are called <u>hard drugs</u>.
2) Almost all users of <u>hard drugs</u> have tried <u>cannabis</u> first because:

1 Using cannabis can make people <u>want</u> to <u>try hard drugs</u>.

Must have OTHER drugs...

2 They meet <u>drug dealers</u> who have hard drugs.

Some Drugs are Legal

1) <u>Smoking</u> and <u>alcohol</u> are both <u>legal</u>.
2) Smoking and alcohol are also <u>harmful</u>:

ALCOHOL causes <u>brain damage</u> and <u>liver damage</u>.

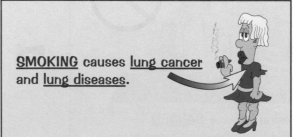

SMOKING causes <u>lung cancer</u> and <u>lung diseases</u>.

3) <u>Legal</u> drugs (smoking and alcohol) have a **<u>BIGGER EFFECT</u>** on the UK's <u>health</u> than <u>illegal drugs</u> (like heroi). This is because <u>a lot more people</u> take <u>legal</u> drugs than take <u>illegal</u> drugs.

Practice Questions

1) Is cannabis a <u>legal</u> or an <u>illegal</u> drug?
2) Give <u>one</u> reason why someone might take <u>cannabis</u>.
3) Give <u>two</u> harmful effects of <u>alcohol</u>.

Adaptations

If you live somewhere <u>hot</u> you need to keep <u>cool</u>. And if you live somewhere <u>cold</u> you need to keep <u>warm</u>.

Animals and Plants are Adapted to Their Environment

1) If an animal or plant is <u>ADAPTED</u> to it's <u>environment</u> it means it's got <u>FEATURES</u> that help it to <u>SURVIVE</u> there.

These features are called <u>adaptations</u>.

2) Here are some <u>examples</u>:

1) Desert Animals Need to Lose Heat

1) Deserts are <u>really HOT</u>. This means that animals living there have features to help them <u>LOSE HEAT</u>.

2) The <u>camel</u> is <u>adapted</u> to living in <u>deserts</u>:

LONG, THIN SHAPE to help <u>lose heat</u>.

THIN COAT of fur to help <u>lose heat</u>.

SANDY COLOUR makes the animal <u>hard to see</u> in the <u>sand</u>. This is called **CAMOUFLAGE**.

VERY LITTLE BODY FAT to help <u>lose heat</u>.

2) Arctic Animals Need to Save Heat

1) <u>The arctic</u> is <u>really COLD</u>. This means animals living there have features to help them <u>KEEP HEAT IN</u>.

2) The <u>polar bear</u> is <u>adapted</u> to living in <u>the arctic</u>:

ROUND SHAPE to help <u>keep heat in</u>.

THICK COAT of fur to help <u>keep heat in</u>.

LOTS OF BODY FAT to help <u>keep heat in</u>.

WHITE FUR for <u>camouflage</u>.

Practice Questions

1) What does it mean if an animal is <u>adapted to its environment</u>?
2) Give <u>two</u> features of a <u>camel</u> that help it to live in the <u>desert</u>.
3) Give <u>two</u> features of a <u>polar bear</u> that help it to live in the <u>arctic</u>.

Adaptations

Here are some more <u>examples</u> of how <u>plants</u> and <u>animals</u> have <u>adapted</u> to their <u>environment</u>.

③ *Desert Plants Need to Save Water*

1) Deserts are <u>VERY DRY</u>. This means that plants living there have features to help them <u>SAVE WATER</u>.

2) The <u>cactus</u> is adapted to living in <u>deserts</u>:

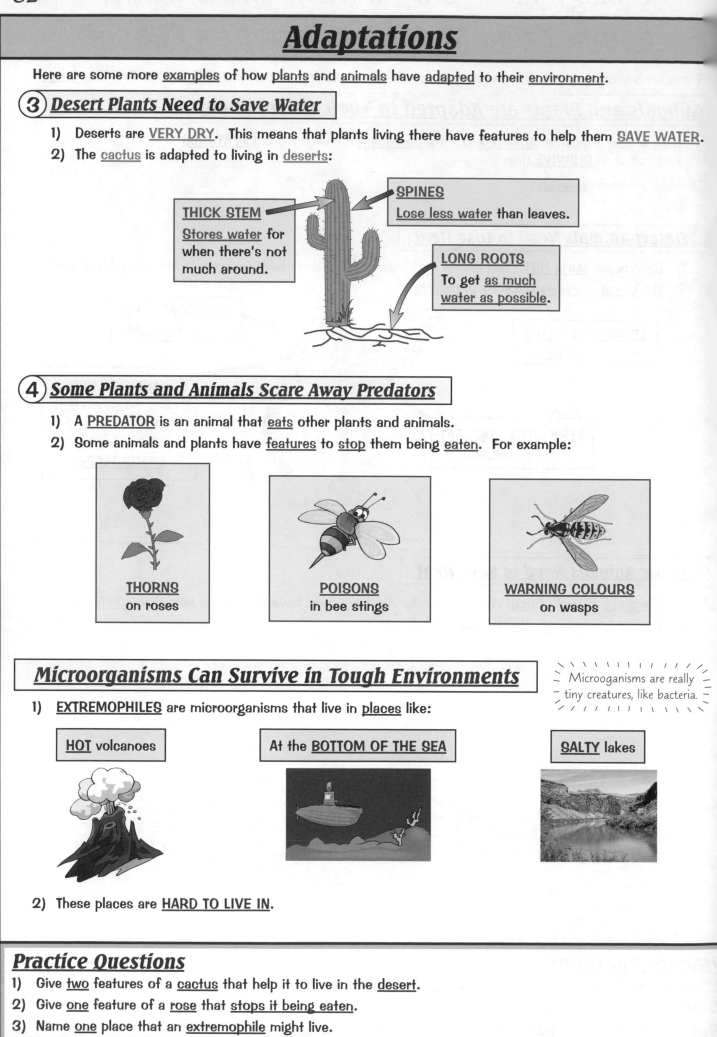

SPINES
Lose less water than leaves.

THICK STEM
<u>Stores water</u> for when there's not much around.

LONG ROOTS
To get <u>as much water as possible</u>.

④ *Some Plants and Animals Scare Away Predators*

1) A <u>PREDATOR</u> is an animal that <u>eats</u> other plants and animals.

2) Some animals and plants have <u>features</u> to <u>stop</u> them being <u>eaten</u>. For example:

THORNS
on roses

POISONS
in bee stings

WARNING COLOURS
on wasps

Microorganisms Can Survive in Tough Environments

Microorganisms are really tiny creatures, like bacteria.

1) <u>EXTREMOPHILES</u> are microorganisms that live in <u>places</u> like:

<u>HOT</u> volcanoes

At the <u>BOTTOM OF THE SEA</u>

<u>SALTY</u> lakes

2) These places are <u>HARD TO LIVE IN</u>.

Practice Questions

1) Give <u>two</u> features of a <u>cactus</u> that help it to live in the <u>desert</u>.

2) Give <u>one</u> feature of a <u>rose</u> that <u>stops it being eaten</u>.

3) Name <u>one</u> place that an <u>extremophile</u> might live.

Competition and Environmental Change

Animals and plants need things like <u>food</u> and <u>water</u> to <u>stay alive</u>. If there <u>aren't enough</u> of these things where they are, they might have to <u>go somewhere else</u> to find them.

Plants and Animals Fight For the Things They Need

1) An <u>ORGANISM</u> is a <u>plant</u> or an <u>animal</u>.

2) Organisms <u>need</u> these things to <u>survive</u> and <u>breed</u>:

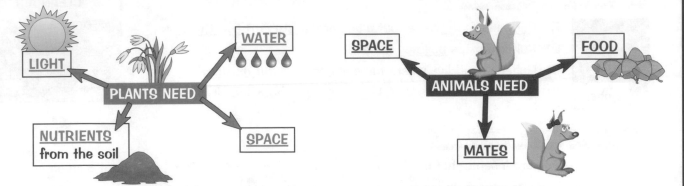

3) Organisms get some of these things from <u>around them</u>. For example, <u>water</u> and <u>light</u>.

4) They get some of these things from <u>other living things</u>. For example, <u>mates</u> and <u>food</u>.

5) Organisms <u>COMPETE</u> (<u>fight</u>) with each other for the things they need.

Changes in the Environment are Caused by Different Things

1) The <u>environment</u> that a plant or animal lives in can <u>change over time</u>.

2) The change could be caused by another <u>LIVING THING</u>.

> For example, owls and foxes <u>compete for food</u>. If the <u>number of owls goes up</u>, they will eat <u>more food</u>. This means there will be <u>less food</u> for the foxes.

3) The change could also be caused by a <u>NON-LIVING THING</u>.

> For example, if more <u>rain</u> falls there will be <u>more water</u> in the soil for <u>plants</u>.

Changes in the Environment Can Affect Plants and Animals

1) <u>Changes in the environment</u> can make the <u>NUMBER</u> of plants or animals go <u>UP</u> or <u>DOWN</u>.
   For example, <u>disease</u> could be causing the number of <u>bees</u> in the USA to <u>go down</u>.

2) <u>Changes in the environment</u> can also change <u>WHERE</u> plants or animals live. For example:

Some birds like to live in <u>warm</u> areas.

The cool area gets <u>warmer</u>.

The birds <u>move</u> into that area.

Practice Questions

1) Name <u>two</u> things that <u>plants</u> need.

2) Name <u>two</u> things that <u>animals</u> need.

Measuring Environmental Change

Environments are <u>changing</u> all the time. Some of these changes can be <u>measured</u>.

You Can Measure Environmental Changes Using Living Indicators...

1) <u>LIVING INDICATORS</u> are organisms that are <u>affected</u> by <u>CHANGES</u> in their environment.
2) They can be used to show <u>how much pollution</u> there is somewhere. For example:

LOTS OF LICHEN = CLEAN AIR

1) <u>Cars</u> and <u>factories</u> let out a <u>gas</u> called <u>SULFUR DIOXIDE</u>.
2) Sulfur dioxide <u>pollutes</u> the air.
3) <u>Lichens can't live</u> where there is <u>lots of sulfur dioxide</u>.
4) This means if there is <u>LOTS OF LICHEN</u> about the air is <u>CLEAN</u>.

Lichen

CLEAN AIR

lich

MAYFLY LARVAE = CLEAN WATER

1) <u>Mayfly larvae</u> are insects that live in water.
2) They need <u>lots of oxygen</u> to live.
3) <u>Clean water</u> has <u>lots of oxygen</u> in it.
4) This means if you find <u>MAYFLY LARVAE</u> in a river you know the water is <u>CLEAN</u>.

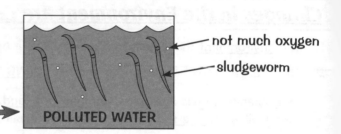

lots of oxygen

mayfly larvae

CLEAN WATER

SLUDGEWORMS = POLLUTED WATER

1) <u>Sludgeworms</u> are tiny worms that live in water.
2) They <u>don't need much oxygen</u> to live.
3) <u>Polluted water doesn't have much oxygen</u> in it.
4) This means if you find <u>SLUDGEWORMS</u> in a river you know the water is <u>POLLUTED</u>.

not much oxygen

sludgeworm

POLLUTED WATER

...and Non-Living Indicators

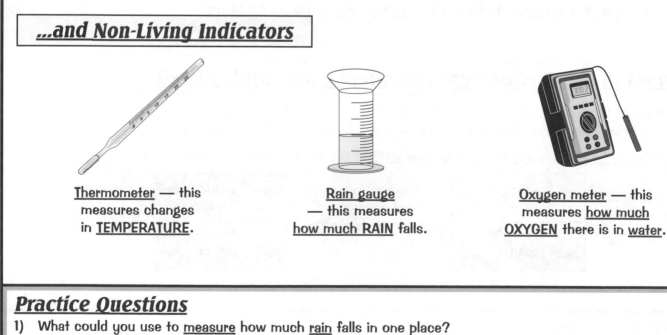

<u>Thermometer</u> — this measures changes in **TEMPERATURE**.

<u>Rain gauge</u> — this measures <u>how much RAIN</u> falls.

<u>Oxygen meter</u> — this measures <u>how much</u> **OXYGEN** there is in <u>water</u>.

Practice Questions

1) What could you use to <u>measure</u> how much <u>rain</u> falls in one place?
2) What does it mean if you find lots of <u>lichen</u> in an area?
3) What does it mean if you find lots of <u>sludgeworms</u> in a river?

Pyramids of Biomass

All animals need to <u>eat</u> to stay alive. Eating makes you part of a <u>food chain</u>.

A Food Chain Shows What is Eaten By What

For example, this is a food chain:

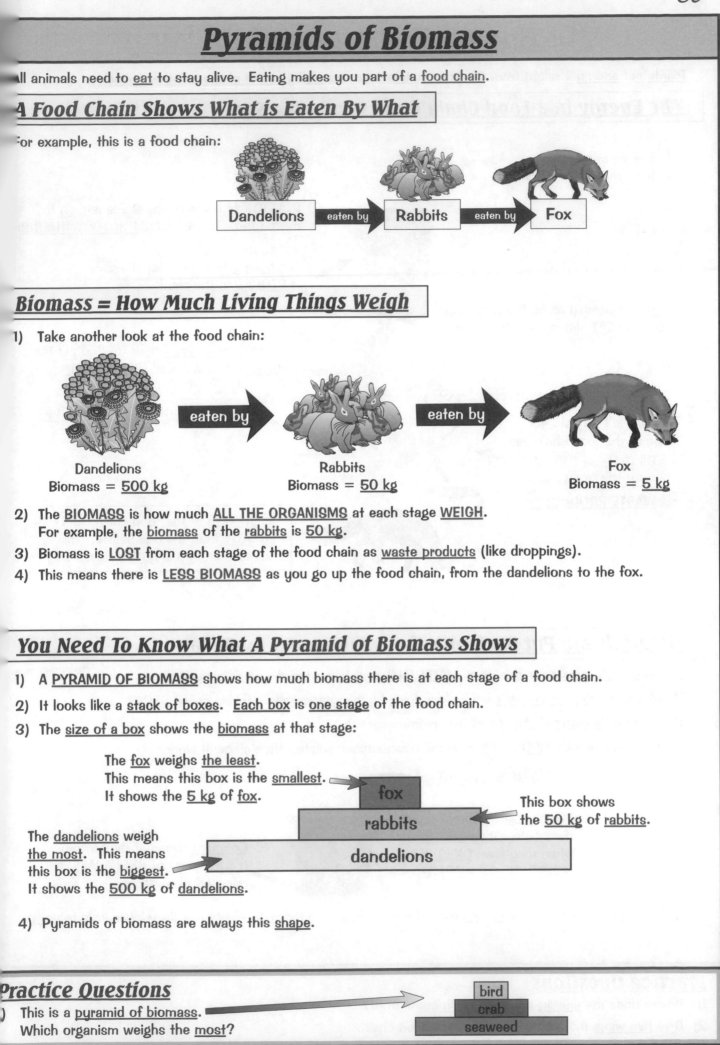

| Dandelions | eaten by | Rabbits | eaten by | Fox |

Biomass = How Much Living Things Weigh

1) Take another look at the food chain:

Dandelions
Biomass = <u>500 kg</u>

eaten by

Rabbits
Biomass = <u>50 kg</u>

eaten by

Fox
Biomass = <u>5 kg</u>

2) The <u>BIOMASS</u> is how much <u>ALL THE ORGANISMS</u> at each stage <u>WEIGH</u>. For example, the <u>biomass</u> of the <u>rabbits</u> is <u>50 kg</u>.

3) Biomass is <u>LOST</u> from each stage of the food chain as <u>waste products</u> (like droppings).

4) This means there is <u>LESS BIOMASS</u> as you go up the food chain, from the dandelions to the fox.

You Need To Know What A Pyramid of Biomass Shows

1) A <u>PYRAMID OF BIOMASS</u> shows how much biomass there is at each stage of a food chain.

2) It looks like a <u>stack of boxes</u>. <u>Each box</u> is <u>one stage</u> of the food chain.

3) The <u>size of a box</u> shows the <u>biomass</u> at that stage:

The <u>fox</u> weighs <u>the least</u>.
This means this box is the <u>smallest</u>.
It shows the <u>5 kg</u> of <u>fox</u>.

fox

This box shows
the <u>50 kg</u> of <u>rabbits</u>.

rabbits

The <u>dandelions</u> weigh <u>the most</u>. This means this box is the <u>biggest</u>. It shows the <u>500 kg</u> of <u>dandelions</u>.

dandelions

4) Pyramids of biomass are always this <u>shape</u>.

Practice Questions

) This is a <u>pyramid of biomass</u>.
Which organism weighs the <u>most</u>?

bird
crab
seaweed

Energy Transfer and Decay

<u>Plants</u> get <u>energy</u> straight from the <u>Sun</u>. <u>Animals</u> get energy by <u>eating plants</u> or <u>other animals</u>...

The Energy in a Food Chain Comes From the Sun

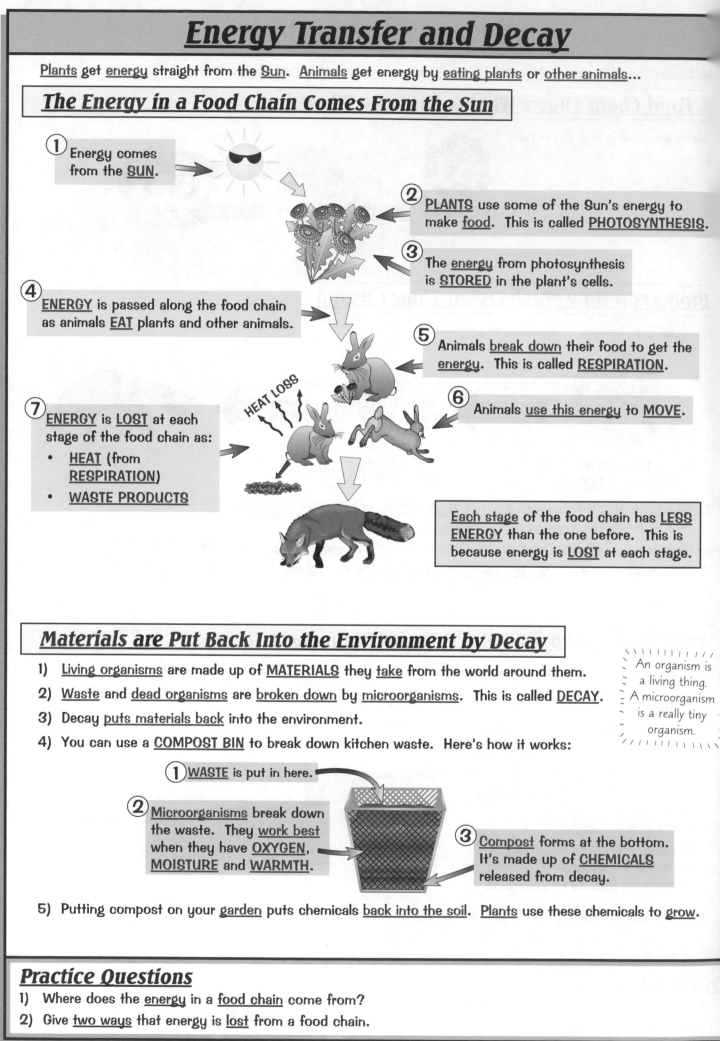

① Energy comes from the <u>SUN</u>.

② <u>PLANTS</u> use some of the Sun's energy to make <u>food</u>. This is called <u>PHOTOSYNTHESIS</u>.

③ The <u>energy</u> from photosynthesis is <u>STORED</u> in the plant's cells.

④ <u>ENERGY</u> is passed along the food chain as animals <u>EAT</u> plants and other animals.

⑤ Animals <u>break down</u> their food to get the <u>energy</u>. This is called <u>RESPIRATION</u>.

⑥ Animals <u>use this energy</u> to <u>MOVE</u>.

HEAT LOSS

⑦ <u>ENERGY</u> is <u>LOST</u> at each stage of the food chain as:
- <u>HEAT</u> (from <u>RESPIRATION</u>)
- <u>WASTE PRODUCTS</u>

Each stage of the food chain has <u>LESS ENERGY</u> than the one before. This is because energy is <u>LOST</u> at each stage.

Materials are Put Back Into the Environment by Decay

1) <u>Living organisms</u> are made up of <u>MATERIALS</u> they <u>take</u> from the world around them.

2) <u>Waste</u> and <u>dead organisms</u> are <u>broken down</u> by <u>microorganisms</u>. This is called <u>DECAY</u>.

3) Decay <u>puts materials back</u> into the environment.

4) You can use a <u>COMPOST BIN</u> to break down kitchen waste. Here's how it works:

An organism is a living thing. A microorganism is a really tiny organism.

① <u>WASTE</u> is put in here.

② <u>Microorganisms</u> break down the waste. They <u>work best</u> when they have <u>OXYGEN</u>, <u>MOISTURE</u> and <u>WARMTH</u>.

③ <u>Compost</u> forms at the bottom. It's made up of <u>CHEMICALS</u> released from decay.

5) Putting compost on your <u>garden</u> puts chemicals <u>back into the soil</u>. <u>Plants</u> use these chemicals to <u>grow</u>.

Practice Questions

1) Where does the <u>energy</u> in a <u>food chain</u> come from?

2) Give <u>two ways</u> that energy is <u>lost</u> from a food chain.

The Carbon Cycle

Lots of people don't like the carbon cycle, but I happen to love it. I hope you will too...

The Carbon Cycle Shows How Carbon is Recycled

1) CARBON is in lots of different things. For example, plants, animals and animal poo.

2) Carbon can move between these things. The carbon cycle shows this:

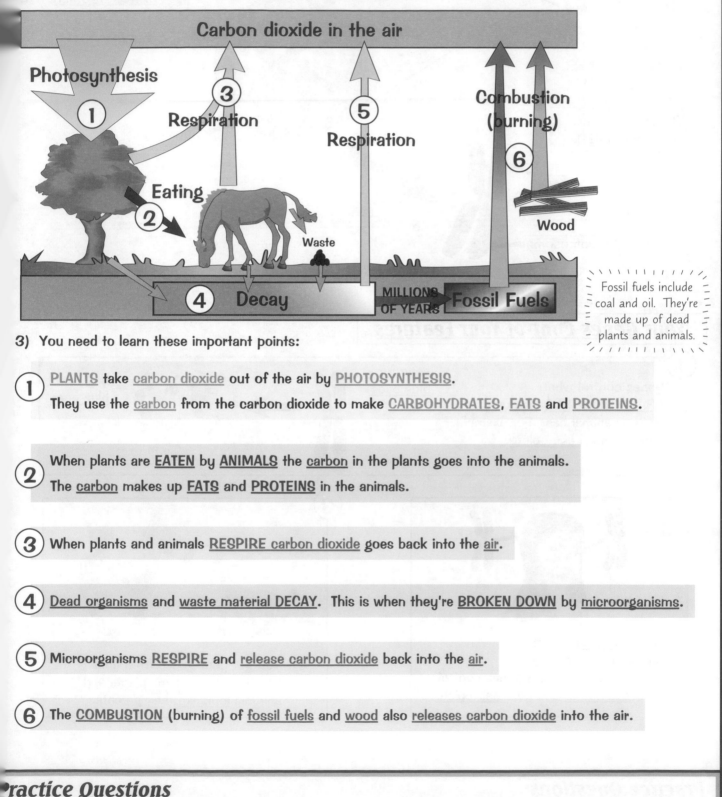

3) You need to learn these important points:

1 PLANTS take carbon dioxide out of the air by PHOTOSYNTHESIS.
   They use the carbon from the carbon dioxide to make CARBOHYDRATES, FATS and PROTEINS.

2 When plants are EATEN by ANIMALS the carbon in the plants goes into the animals.
   The carbon makes up FATS and PROTEINS in the animals.

3 When plants and animals RESPIRE carbon dioxide goes back into the air.

4 Dead organisms and waste material DECAY. This is when they're BROKEN DOWN by microorganisms.

5 Microorganisms RESPIRE and release carbon dioxide back into the air.

6 The COMBUSTION (burning) of fossil fuels and wood also releases carbon dioxide into the air.

Practice Questions

1) "The carbon cycle shows how carbon is recycled." True or false?

2) How do plants take carbon dioxide out of the air?

3) Give two ways carbon is released into the air.

Genes and Chromosomes

It's <u>dead important</u> you get to grips with all the stuff on this page.

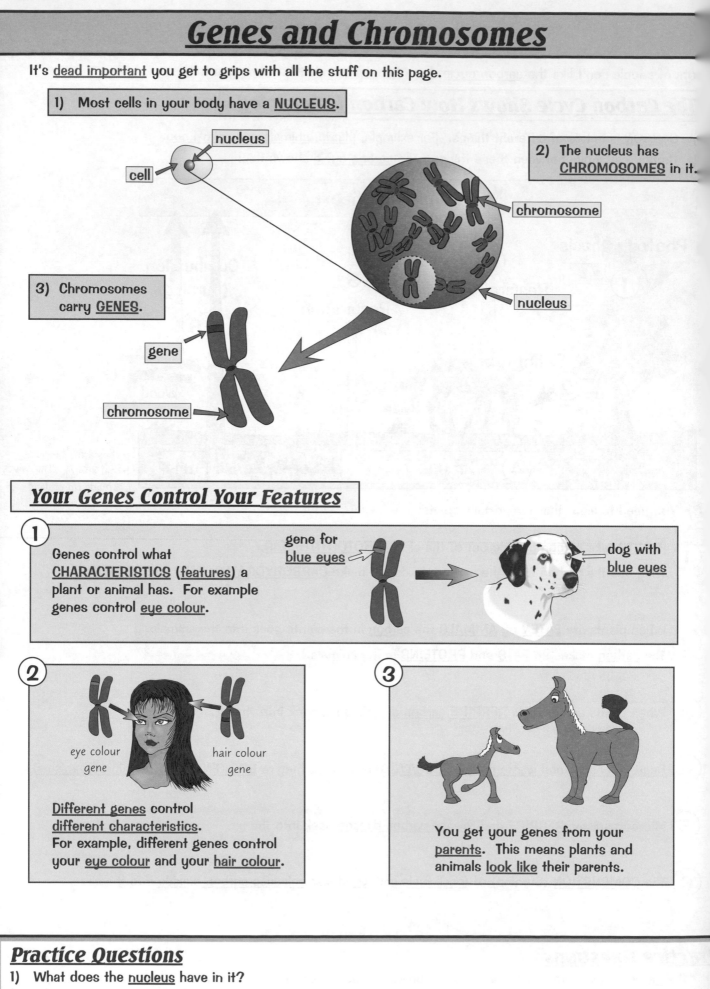

1) Most cells in your body have a <u>NUCLEUS</u>.

nucleus

cell

2) The nucleus has <u>CHROMOSOMES</u> in it.

chromosome

nucleus

3) Chromosomes carry <u>GENES</u>.

gene

chromosome

Your Genes Control Your Features

1 Genes control what <u>CHARACTERISTICS</u> (features) a plant or animal has. For example genes control <u>eye colour</u>.

gene for <u>blue eyes</u>

dog with <u>blue eyes</u>

2 eye colour gene

hair colour gene

<u>Different genes</u> control <u>different characteristics</u>. For example, different genes control your <u>eye colour</u> and your <u>hair colour</u>.

3 You get your genes from your <u>parents</u>. This means plants and animals <u>look like</u> their parents.

Practice Questions

1) What does the <u>nucleus</u> have in it?
2) "The <u>same genes</u> control your <u>eye colour</u> and your <u>hair colour</u>." True or false?
3) Where do you get your <u>genes</u> from?

Variation

You might have noticed that not everyone <u>looks the same</u>. There are reasons for this.

There Are Differences Between Living Things

1) Plants and animals of the <u>same kind</u> have different <u>characteristics</u>. For example different people have different hair colour.

2) These <u>differences</u> in characteristics are called <u>VARIATION</u>.

3) Variation can be caused by your <u>genes</u>, <u>the environment</u> or <u>both</u>.

1) Genes

1) Some <u>characteristics</u> are controlled <u>only</u> by <u>GENES</u>.

2) You get a <u>mixture</u> of genes passed on to you by your <u>mother</u> and <u>father</u>.

3) This means that <u>everyone</u> ends up with <u>different GENES</u>.

4) Different genes mean we have <u>different characteristics</u>, for example different <u>eye colours</u>.

I got blue eyes from my Dad

I got green eyes from my Mum

2) The Environment

Some characteristics are controlled by the <u>ENVIRONMENT</u>. For example, <u>leaf colour</u>:

A plant grown in the <u>sun</u> will have <u>green leaves</u>.

A plant grown in the <u>dark</u> will have <u>yellow leaves</u>.

3) Genes and the Environment

Most characteristics are affected by <u>BOTH</u> genes and the environment. For example, the <u>height of a plant</u>:

This plant is <u>TALL</u> because:
- It gets <u>lots of sunshine</u>.
- It has <u>genes</u> that make it <u>tall</u>.

Practice Questions

1) "Differences in characteristics are called <u>variation</u>." True or false?

2) Give <u>one characteristic</u> that is controlled by <u>genes</u>.

3) Give <u>one characteristic</u> that is affected by both <u>genes and the environment</u>.

Biology 1b — Environment and Evolution

Reproduction

Prepare yourself — this page is about <u>making babies</u>. (Well, it had to come up at some point.)

Reproduction Means Making Offspring

There are two types of reproduction you need to know about:

Offspring means children.

① Sexual Reproduction

1) Adult males and females have <u>sex cells</u>. These are called <u>GAMETES</u>.

2) In animals the <u>female gamete</u> is the <u>egg</u>. And the <u>male gamete</u> is the <u>sperm</u>.

3) The egg and sperm <u>fuse</u> (join together) to produce a <u>new cell</u>.

4) The <u>new cell</u> will <u>grow</u> into a <u>baby animal</u>. This is called <u>SEXUAL REPRODUCTION</u>.

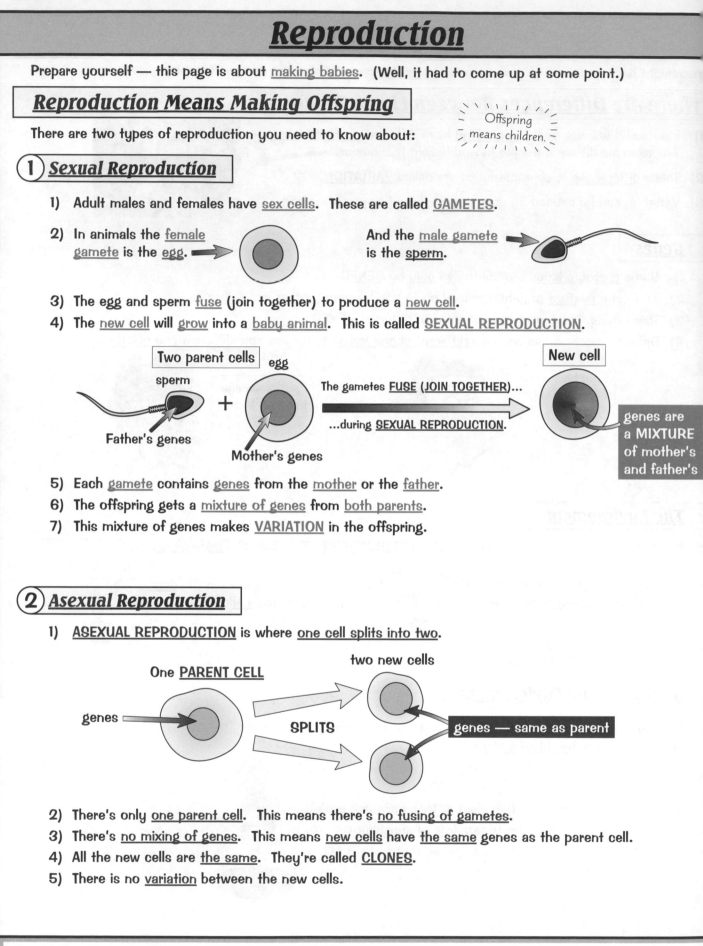

Two parent cells
sperm   egg
Father's genes
Mother's genes

The gametes <u>FUSE (JOIN TOGETHER)</u>...
...during <u>SEXUAL REPRODUCTION</u>.

New cell
genes are a MIXTURE of mother's and father's

5) Each <u>gamete</u> contains <u>genes</u> from the <u>mother</u> or the <u>father</u>.
6) The offspring gets a <u>mixture of genes</u> from <u>both parents</u>.
7) This mixture of genes makes <u>VARIATION</u> in the offspring.

② Asexual Reproduction

1) <u>ASEXUAL REPRODUCTION</u> is where <u>one cell splits into two</u>.

One <u>PARENT CELL</u>
genes
SPLITS
two new cells
genes — same as parent

2) There's only <u>one parent cell</u>. This means there's <u>no fusing of gametes</u>.
3) There's <u>no mixing of genes</u>. This means <u>new cells</u> have <u>the same</u> genes as the parent cell.
4) All the new cells are <u>the same</u>. They're called <u>CLONES</u>.
5) There is no <u>variation</u> between the new cells.

Practice Questions

1) What is the <u>male gamete</u> in animals?
2) How many parent cells are needed for <u>sexual reproduction</u>?
3) Does <u>asexual reproduction</u> make cells that are <u>the same</u> or cells that are <u>different</u>?

Cloning

There are a few different ways to make a <u>copy</u> of a <u>plant</u> or an <u>animal</u>.

You Can Clone Plants

1) You can make a <u>copy</u> of a <u>plant</u> — this is called a <u>CLONE</u>.

2) <u>Clones</u> have exactly the <u>SAME GENES</u> as each other.

3) You can <u>clone a plant</u> by <u>TAKING CUTTINGS</u> from it:

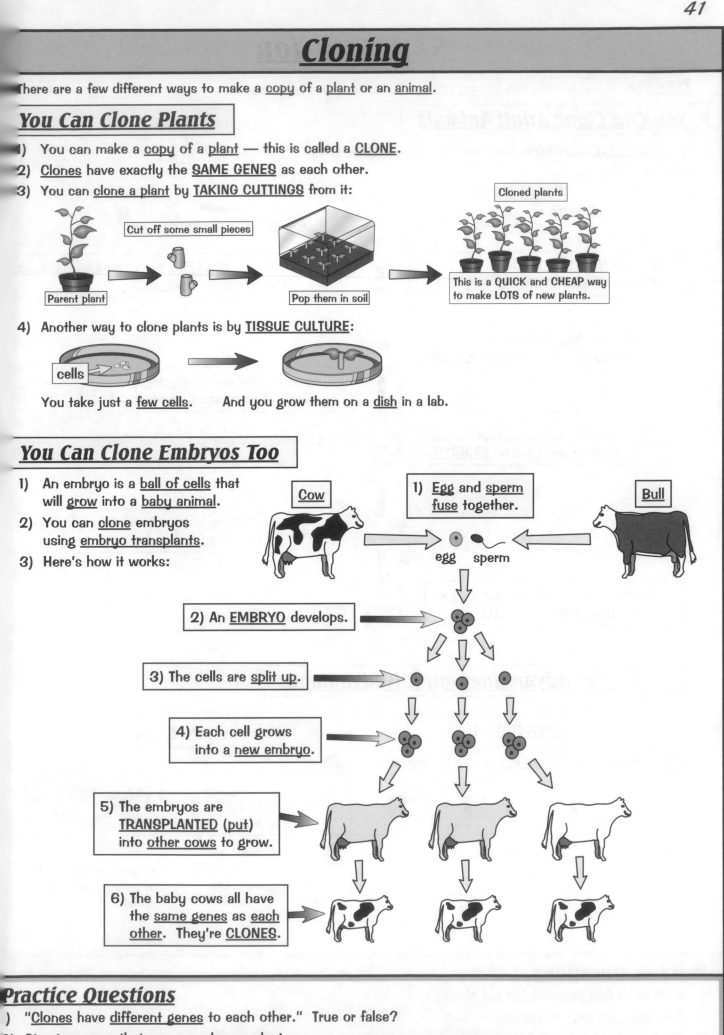

Cut off some small pieces

Parent plant

Pop them in soil

Cloned plants

This is a QUICK and CHEAP way to make LOTS of new plants.

4) Another way to clone plants is by <u>TISSUE CULTURE</u>:

cells

You take just a <u>few cells</u>.   And you grow them on a <u>dish</u> in a lab.

You Can Clone Embryos Too

1) An embryo is a <u>ball of cells</u> that will <u>grow</u> into a <u>baby animal</u>.

2) You can <u>clone</u> embryos using <u>embryo transplants</u>.

3) Here's how it works:

Cow

Bull

1) <u>Egg</u> and <u>sperm</u> <u>fuse</u> together.

egg   sperm

2) An <u>EMBRYO</u> develops.

3) The cells are <u>split up</u>.

4) Each cell grows into a <u>new embryo</u>.

5) The embryos are <u>TRANSPLANTED</u> (put) into <u>other cows</u> to grow.

6) The baby cows all have the <u>same genes</u> as <u>each other</u>. They're <u>CLONES</u>.

Practice Questions

1) "<u>Clones</u> have <u>different genes</u> to each other." True or false?

2) Give <u>two ways</u> that you can <u>clone a plant</u>.

Cloning

Cloning plants and animals can be very useful. But it can cause problems too.

You Can Clone Adult Animals

1) ADULT CELL CLONING is how scientists clone adult animals.

2) This is how it works:

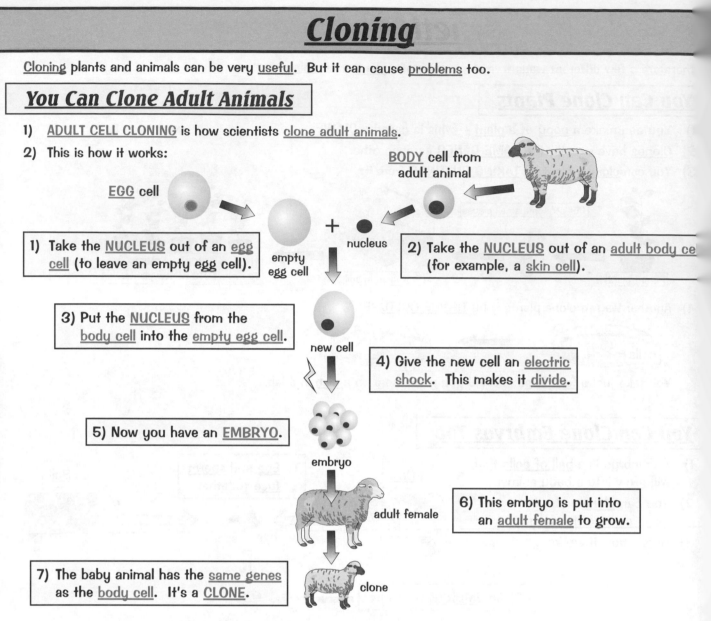

EGG cell

BODY cell from adult animal

1) Take the NUCLEUS out of an egg cell (to leave an empty egg cell).

empty egg cell

nucleus

2) Take the NUCLEUS out of an adult body ce (for example, a skin cell).

3) Put the NUCLEUS from the body cell into the empty egg cell.

new cell

4) Give the new cell an electric shock. This makes it divide.

5) Now you have an EMBRYO.

embryo

adult female

6) This embryo is put into an adult female to grow.

7) The baby animal has the same genes as the body cell. It's a CLONE.

clone

Cloning Has Advantages and Disadvantages

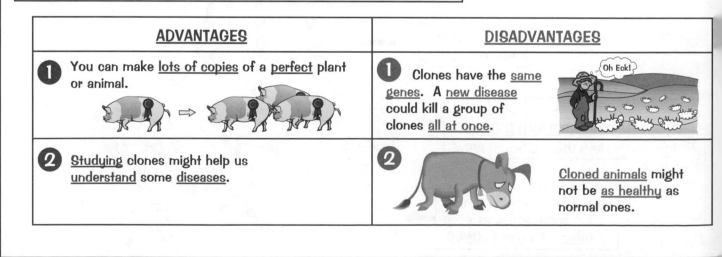

ADVANTAGES	DISADVANTAGES
1 You can make lots of copies of a perfect plant or animal.	1 Clones have the same genes. A new disease could kill a group of clones all at once.
2 Studying clones might help us understand some diseases.	2 Cloned animals might not be as healthy as normal ones.

Practice Questions

1) What's the first step in adult cell cloning?

2) Give one advantage of cloning.

3) Give one disadvantage of cloning.

Biology 1b — Environment and Evolution

Genetic Engineering

If you <u>change</u> a living thing's <u>genes</u> you can give it <u>new characteristics</u> (features).

Genetic Engineering Means Cutting and Pasting Genes

Here's how genetic engineering works:

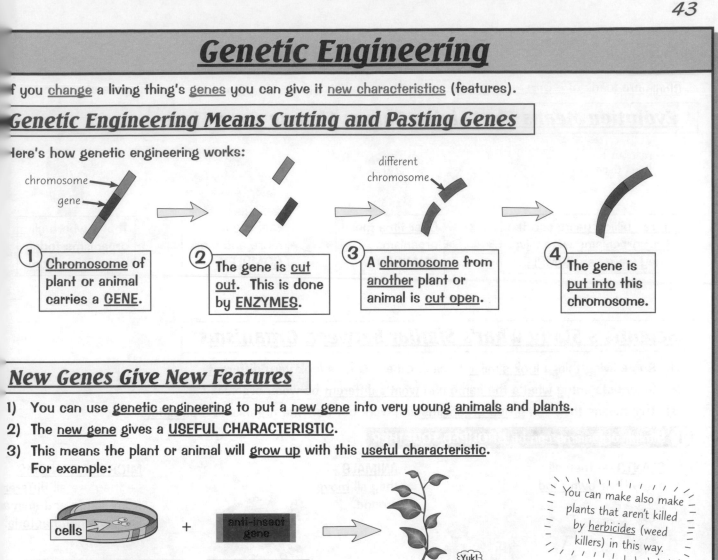

① **Chromosome** of plant or animal carries a **GENE**.

② The gene is <u>cut out</u>. This is done by **ENZYMES**.

③ A <u>chromosome</u> from <u>another</u> plant or animal is <u>cut open</u>.

④ The gene is <u>put into</u> this chromosome.

New Genes Give New Features

1) You can use <u>genetic engineering</u> to put a <u>new gene</u> into very young <u>animals</u> and <u>plants</u>.

2) The <u>new gene</u> gives a **USEFUL CHARACTERISTIC**.

3) This means the plant or animal will <u>grow up</u> with this <u>useful characteristic</u>.
   For example:

cells	+	anti-insect gene	→	The cells grow into a plant that <u>insects can't attack</u>.
Take the cells of a <u>crop plant</u>. For example a <u>wheat plant</u>.		Add a gene that <u>stops insects eating</u> the plant.		

You can make also make plants that aren't killed by <u>herbicides</u> (weed killers) in this way.

4) <u>Crop plants</u> whose <u>genes</u> have been <u>changed</u> are called <u>genetically modified (GM)</u> <u>crops</u>.

GM Crops Have Advantages and Disadvantages

ADVANTAGES	DISADVANTAGES
① You can add <u>vitamins</u> to GM crops. **GM Rice** With lots of vitamin A	① GM crops could <u>affect</u> the <u>number</u> of <u>flowers</u> and <u>insects</u> nearby. Normal / GM
② GM crops have a <u>higher yield</u> than normal crops. This means we get <u>more food</u> from GM crops. Flour / GM Flour	② Some people think GM crops are <u>not</u> safe to eat. BREAD Tasty white bread made from GM crops.

Practice Questions

1) In <u>genetic engineering</u> a gene is cut out. What is this done by?

2) Give <u>one advantage</u> of <u>GM crops</u>.

3) Give <u>one disadvantage</u> of <u>GM crops</u>.

Evolution

There are loads of <u>different plants and animals</u> around today. <u>Evolution</u> is how they all came about.

Evolution Means That Living Things Change Over Time

An organism is just a living thing.

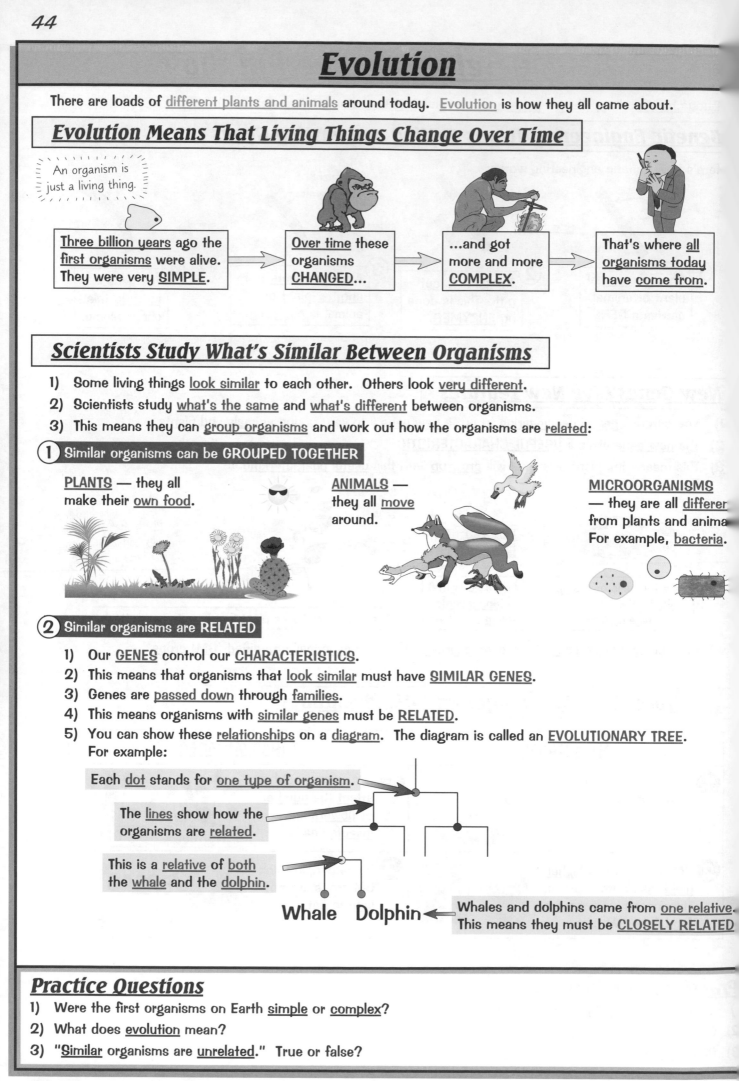

| Three billion years ago the <u>first organisms</u> were alive. They were very <u>SIMPLE</u>. | Over time these organisms <u>CHANGED</u>... | ...and got more and more <u>COMPLEX</u>. | That's where <u>all organisms today</u> have <u>come from</u>. |

Scientists Study What's Similar Between Organisms

1) Some living things <u>look similar</u> to each other. Others look <u>very different</u>.

2) Scientists study <u>what's the same</u> and <u>what's different</u> between organisms.

3) This means they can <u>group organisms</u> and work out how the organisms are <u>related</u>:

① Similar organisms can be GROUPED TOGETHER

<u>PLANTS</u> — they all make their <u>own food</u>.

<u>ANIMALS</u> — they all <u>move</u> around.

<u>MICROORGANISMS</u> — they are all <u>differen</u>from plants and anima For example, <u>bacteria</u>.

② Similar organisms are RELATED

1) Our <u>GENES</u> control our <u>CHARACTERISTICS</u>.

2) This means that organisms that <u>look similar</u> must have <u>SIMILAR GENES</u>.

3) Genes are <u>passed down</u> through <u>families</u>.

4) This means organisms with <u>similar genes</u> must be <u>RELATED</u>.

5) You can show these <u>relationships</u> on a <u>diagram</u>. The diagram is called an <u>EVOLUTIONARY TREE</u>. For example:

Each <u>dot</u> stands for <u>one type of organism</u>.

The <u>lines</u> show how the organisms are <u>related</u>.

This is a <u>relative</u> of <u>both</u> the <u>whale</u> and the <u>dolphin</u>.

Whale   Dolphin

Whales and dolphins came from <u>one relative</u>. This means they must be <u>CLOSELY RELATED</u>

Practice Questions

1) Were the first organisms on Earth <u>simple</u> or <u>complex</u>?

2) What does <u>evolution</u> mean?

3) "<u>Similar</u> organisms are <u>unrelated</u>." True or false?

Natural Selection and Mutations

Natural selection is about how living things pass on useful characteristics to their children.

Natural Selection is How Evolution Happens

A man called CHARLES DARWIN came up with the idea of NATURAL SELECTION. Here's how it works:

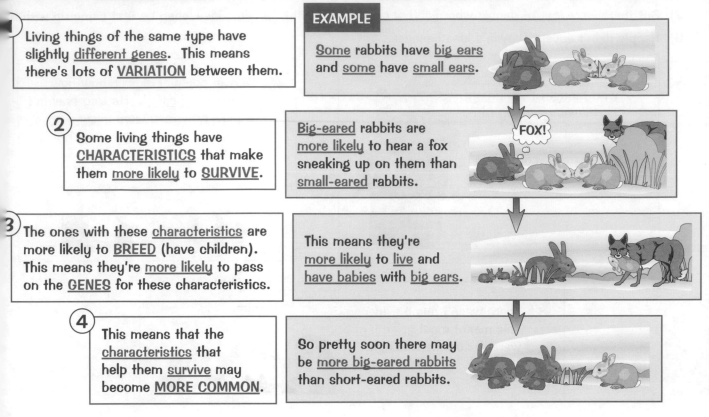

1) Living things of the same type have slightly different genes. This means there's lots of VARIATION between them.

EXAMPLE

Some rabbits have big ears and some have small ears.

2) Some living things have CHARACTERISTICS that make them more likely to SURVIVE.

Big-eared rabbits are more likely to hear a fox sneaking up on them than small-eared rabbits.

FOX!

3) The ones with these characteristics are more likely to BREED (have children). This means they're more likely to pass on the GENES for these characteristics.

This means they're more likely to live and have babies with big ears.

4) This means that the characteristics that help them survive may become MORE COMMON.

So pretty soon there may be more big-eared rabbits than short-eared rabbits.

Genes Can Change Because of Mutations

1) A mutation is a change in a gene.

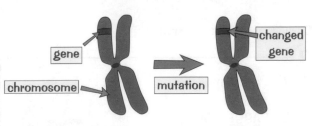

gene

chromosome

mutation

changed gene

2) It can produce a useful characteristic in a plant or an animal.

no mutation

mutation

Rabbit is born with small ears.

Rabbit is born with big ears.

3) The useful characteristic may help the animal or plant to survive in its environment.

4) If the animal or plant survives then the useful characteristic is more likely to be passed on to its children. This happens by NATURAL SELECTION (see above).

Practice Questions

1) Who came up with the idea of natural selection?

2) "Some living things have characteristics that make them more likely to survive". True or false?

3) What is a mutation?

More About Evolution

Living things <u>change</u> over time. <u>Darwin</u> came up with the idea of how this happens.

Not Everyone Agreed with Darwin...

1) Darwin came up with the idea of <u>evolution by natural selection</u>.

2) But there were <u>lots of people</u> who <u>didn't accept</u> (agree with) Darwin's idea when he first came up with it

3) People didn't accept Darwin's idea because...

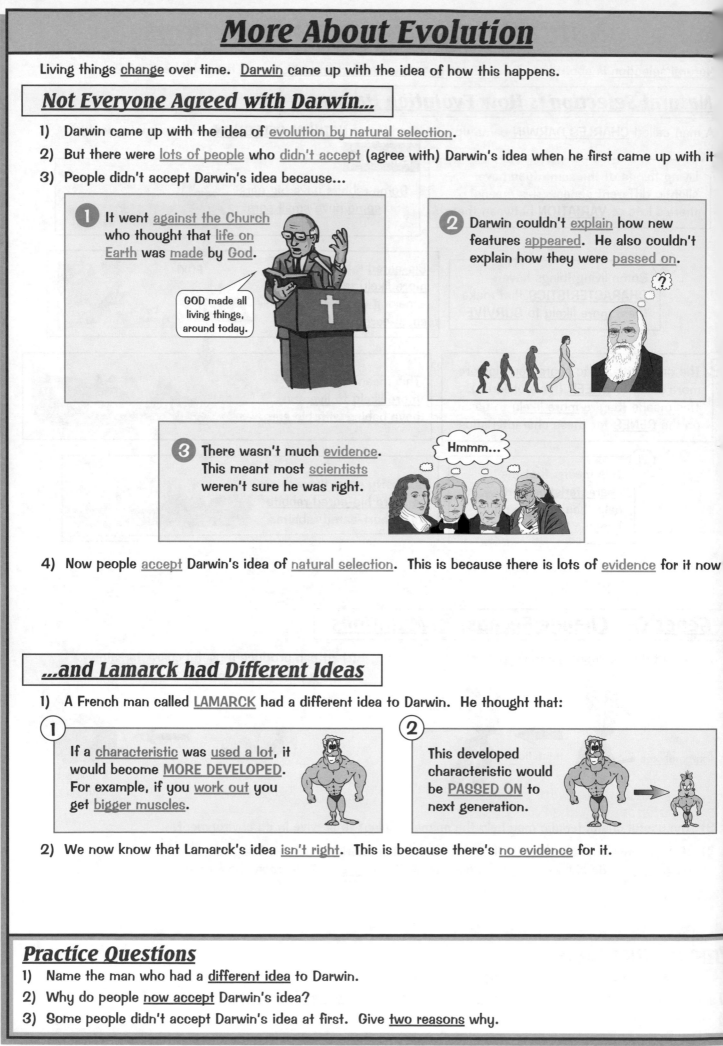

1 It went <u>against the Church</u> who thought that <u>life on Earth</u> was <u>made</u> by <u>God</u>.

GOD made all living things, around today.

2 Darwin couldn't <u>explain</u> how new features <u>appeared</u>. He also couldn't explain how they were <u>passed on</u>.

3 There wasn't much <u>evidence</u>. This meant most <u>scientists</u> weren't sure he was right.

Hmmm...

4) Now people <u>accept</u> Darwin's idea of <u>natural selection</u>. This is because there is lots of <u>evidence</u> for it now

...and Lamarck had Different Ideas

1) A French man called <u>LAMARCK</u> had a different idea to Darwin. He thought that:

1 If a <u>characteristic</u> was <u>used a lot</u>, it would become MORE DEVELOPED. For example, if you <u>work out</u> you get <u>bigger muscles</u>.

2 This developed characteristic would be <u>PASSED ON</u> to next generation.

2) We now know that Lamarck's idea <u>isn't right</u>. This is because there's <u>no evidence</u> for it.

Practice Questions

1) Name the man who had a <u>different idea</u> to Darwin.

2) Why do people <u>now accept</u> Darwin's idea?

3) Some people didn't accept Darwin's idea at first. Give <u>two reasons</u> why.

Atoms and Elements

Everything is made up of <u>atoms</u>. They're really, really <u>tiny</u>.

Atoms have a Nucleus And Electrons

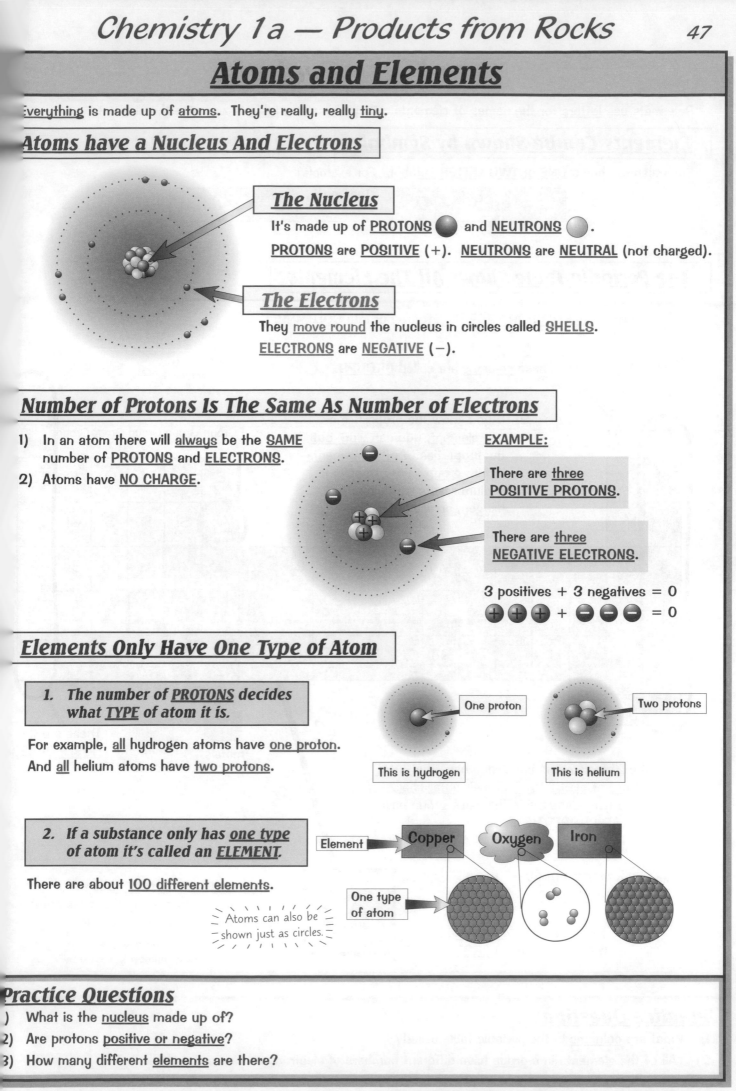

The Nucleus

It's made up of <u>PROTONS</u> ⬤ and <u>NEUTRONS</u> ◯.

<u>PROTONS</u> are <u>POSITIVE</u> (+). <u>NEUTRONS</u> are <u>NEUTRAL</u> (not charged).

The Electrons

They <u>move round</u> the nucleus in circles called <u>SHELLS</u>.

<u>ELECTRONS</u> are <u>NEGATIVE</u> (−).

Number of Protons Is The Same As Number of Electrons

1) In an atom there will <u>always</u> be the <u>SAME</u> number of <u>PROTONS</u> and <u>ELECTRONS</u>.

2) Atoms have <u>NO CHARGE</u>.

EXAMPLE:

There are <u>three</u> POSITIVE PROTONS.

There are <u>three</u> NEGATIVE ELECTRONS.

3 positives + 3 negatives = 0

⊕⊕⊕ + ⊖⊖⊖ = 0

Elements Only Have One Type of Atom

1. The number of <u>PROTONS</u> decides what <u>TYPE</u> of atom it is.

For example, <u>all</u> hydrogen atoms have <u>one proton</u>. And <u>all</u> helium atoms have <u>two protons</u>.

One proton

Two protons

This is hydrogen

This is helium

2. If a substance only has <u>one type</u> of atom it's called an <u>ELEMENT</u>.

There are about <u>100 different elements</u>.

Atoms can also be shown just as circles.

Element

Copper   Oxygen   Iron

One type of atom

Practice Questions

1) What is the <u>nucleus</u> made up of?

2) Are protons <u>positive or negative</u>?

3) How many different <u>elements</u> are there?

The Periodic Table

Scientists use <u>letters</u> for the names of elements. They also use a <u>table</u> to organise the elements.

Elements Can be Shown by Symbols

Each element has a <u>ONE or TWO LETTER</u> symbol. For example:

C = carbon   O = oxygen   Na = sodium

The Periodic Table Shows All The Elements

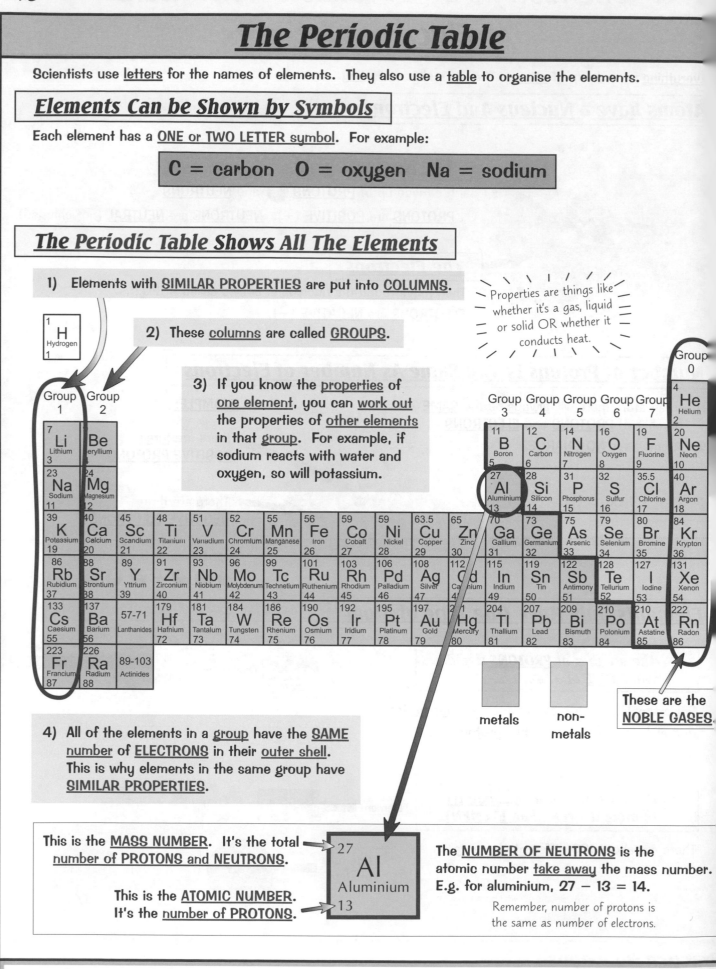

1) Elements with <u>SIMILAR PROPERTIES</u> are put into <u>COLUMNS</u>.

2) These <u>columns</u> are called <u>GROUPS</u>.

Properties are things like whether it's a gas, liquid or solid OR whether it conducts heat.

3) If you know the <u>properties</u> of <u>one element</u>, you can <u>work out</u> the properties of <u>other elements</u> in that <u>group</u>. For example, if sodium reacts with water and oxygen, so will potassium.

These are the <u>NOBLE GASES</u>.

metals   non-metals

4) All of the elements in a <u>group</u> have the <u>SAME number</u> of <u>ELECTRONS</u> in their <u>outer shell</u>. This is why elements in the same group have <u>SIMILAR PROPERTIES</u>.

This is the <u>MASS NUMBER</u>. It's the total number of <u>PROTONS</u> and <u>NEUTRONS</u>.

This is the <u>ATOMIC NUMBER</u>. It's the <u>number of PROTONS</u>.

The <u>NUMBER OF NEUTRONS</u> is the atomic number <u>take away</u> the mass number. E.g. for aluminium, 27 − 13 = 14.

Remember, number of protons is the same as number of electrons.

Practice Questions

1) What are <u>columns</u> in the periodic table called?
2) "All of the elements in a <u>group</u> have different numbers of electrons in their outer shells." True or false?

Electron Shells

Electrons move round the nucleus in <u>shells</u>. You need to learn <u>how many</u> electrons go in each shell.

Electron Shell Rules:

1) Electrons can be found in <u>SHELLS</u>.

FIRST RULE:

The <u>INSIDE</u> shell fills up <u>FIRST</u>.
It takes <u>TWO</u> electrons.

There's only room for two of us in this shell.

1st 2nd 3rd

Electrons can be shown as dots or as crosses.

SECOND RULE:

The <u>other shells</u> can take up to <u>EIGHT</u> electrons.

2) Atoms are much <u>happier</u> when they have a <u>FULL OUTER SHELL</u>. It means they <u>WON'T REACT</u>.
For example, the <u>noble gases</u> all have full outer shells — so they're <u>unreactive</u>.

Follow the Rules to Work Out Electronic Structures

The electronic structure just shows where electrons are found in the shells.

<u>EXAMPLE:</u> <u>Nitrogen</u> has <u>seven</u> protons. That means it's <u>also got 7 electrons</u>.
Follow the 'Electron Shell Rules' to work out its <u>electronic structure</u>.

Step 1:
The <u>INSIDE SHELL</u> can <u>only take 2</u> electrons.

Step 2:
The <u>SECOND SHELL</u> can <u>take up to 8</u> electrons.

<u>TWO</u> of the seven electrons go into the first shell.

The <u>FIVE</u> left over electrons go into the second shell.

You can write out the <u>ELECTRONIC STRUCTURE</u> of <u>nitrogen</u> like this:

2, 5

<u>TWO</u> of the seven electrons go into the first shell.

Don't forget this.

The <u>FIVE</u> left over electrons go into the second shell.

You can use the 'Electron Shell Rules' to work out the electronic structure of any element.

Remember — the number of protons is the same as the number of electrons.

Practice Questions

1) Which <u>shell</u> fills up with electrons first?
2) Use the 'Electron Shell Rules' to write out the <u>electronic structure</u> of argon. Argon has **18** protons.

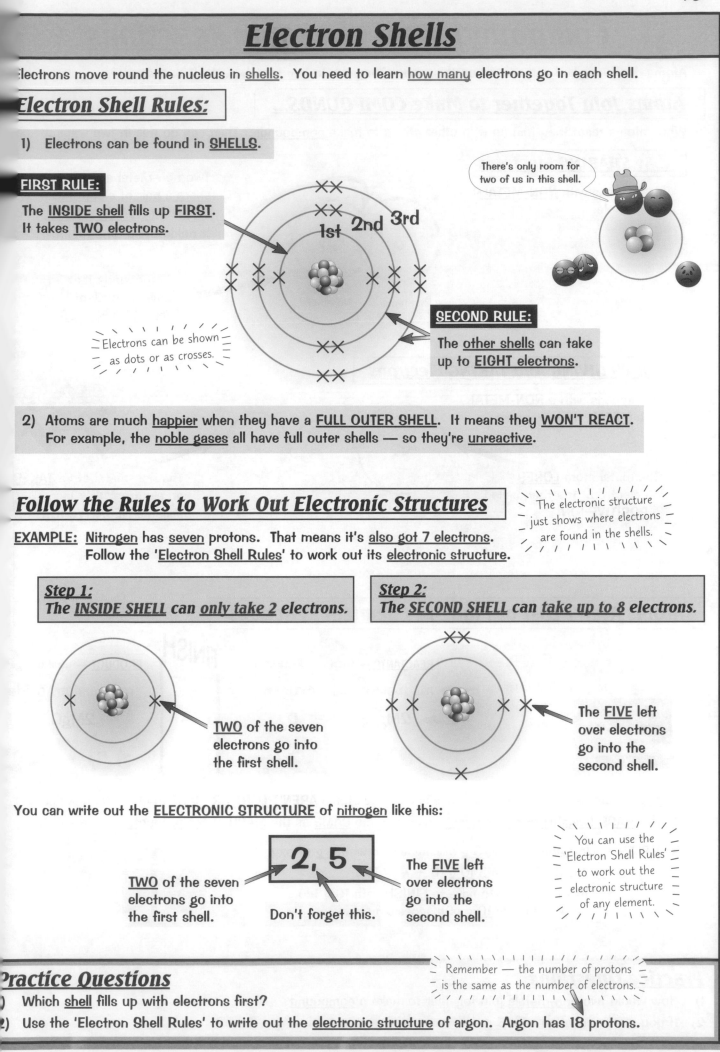

Compounds and Chemical Reactions

Atoms don't usually hang around on their own. They like to join together. Isn't that sweet?

Atoms Join Together to Make COMPOUNDS...

When atoms react they join up with other atoms to make compounds. They can do this in two ways...

...By SHARING Electrons

This happens with NON-METALS. For example:

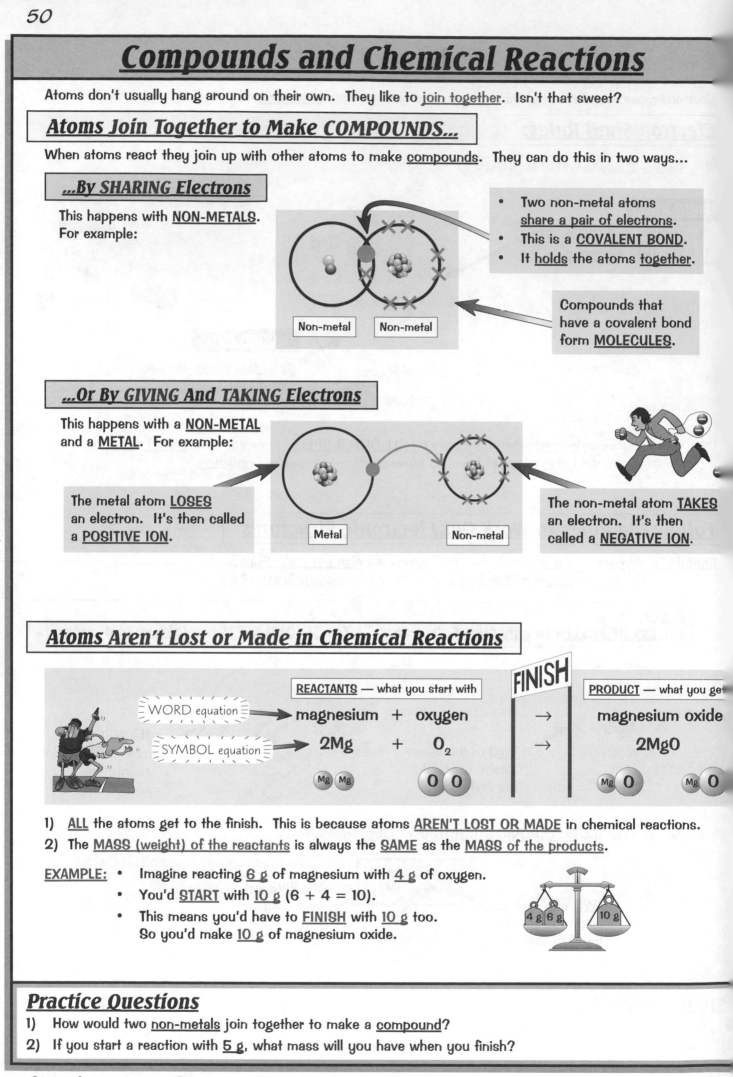

Non-metal   Non-metal

- Two non-metal atoms share a pair of electrons.
- This is a COVALENT BOND.
- It holds the atoms together.

Compounds that have a covalent bond form MOLECULES.

...Or By GIVING And TAKING Electrons

This happens with a NON-METAL and a METAL. For example:

Metal   Non-metal

The metal atom LOSES an electron. It's then called a POSITIVE ION.

The non-metal atom TAKES an electron. It's then called a NEGATIVE ION.

Atoms Aren't Lost or Made in Chemical Reactions

WORD equation → REACTANTS — what you start with

magnesium + oxygen → FINISH → PRODUCT — what you get

magnesium oxide

SYMBOL equation → $2Mg$ + O_2 → $2MgO$

1) ALL the atoms get to the finish. This is because atoms AREN'T LOST OR MADE in chemical reactions.

2) The MASS (weight) of the reactants is always the SAME as the MASS of the products.

EXAMPLE:
- Imagine reacting 6 g of magnesium with 4 g of oxygen.
- You'd START with 10 g (6 + 4 = 10).
- This means you'd have to FINISH with 10 g too. So you'd make 10 g of magnesium oxide.

Practice Questions

1) How would two non-metals join together to make a compound?

2) If you start a reaction with 5 g, what mass will you have when you finish?

Chemistry 1a — Products from Rocks

Limestone

Limestone isn't anything to do with limes. It's a shame because I like limes.

Limestone is Mostly Calcium Carbonate

1) Limestone's <u>QUARRIED</u> (dug up) out of the ground.

2) It's used as a <u>BUILDING MATERIAL</u>.

3) Limestone is mostly <u>CALCIUM CARBONATE</u> (you can write this as $CaCO_3$).

4) If you <u>HEAT calcium carbonate</u>, this happens:

> calcium carbonate $\rightarrow$ calcium oxide + carbon dioxide
>
> **HEAT**

> Calcium carbonate has <u>THERMALLY DECOMPOSED</u> (broken down by heating) into calcium oxide and carbon dioxide.

5) <u>All metal carbonates</u> decompose in the <u>SAME way</u>.

> metal carbonate $\longrightarrow$ metal oxide + carbon dioxide

For example:

> magnesium carbonate $\rightarrow$ magnesium oxide + carbon dioxide

You <u>CAN'T</u> do this to <u>all carbonates</u> using a <u>Bunsen burner</u>. It just <u>doesn't get HOT enough</u> for some of them.

You don't scare me. You're not hot enough.

Carbonates React with Acid

1) <u>CALCIUM CARBONATE</u> reacts with <u>ACID</u> to make a <u>CALCIUM SALT</u>, <u>CARBON DIOXIDE</u> and <u>WATER</u>.

> calcium carbonate + sulfuric acid $\rightarrow$ calcium sulfate + carbon dioxide + water

Carbonate   Acid   A salt

2) This reaction means that <u>buildings and statues</u> made of limestone (calcium carbonate) can be <u>DAMAGED</u> by <u>ACID RAIN</u>.

Carbon dioxide   Acid   Limestone

3) Metal carbonates like <u>magnesium</u>, <u>copper</u>, <u>zinc</u> and <u>sodium</u> carbonates also react with acid to make a <u>SALT</u>, <u>CARBON DIOXIDE</u> and <u>WATER</u>.

> acid + metal carbonate $\longrightarrow$ salt + water + carbon dioxide

Salts aren't always like the salt you put on chips.

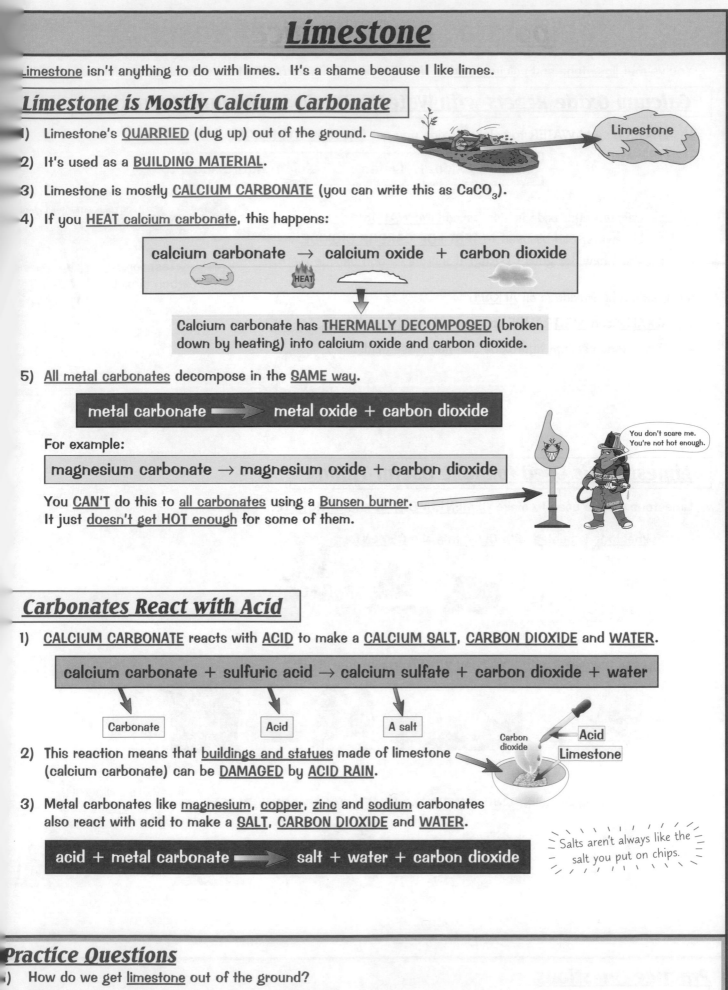

Practice Questions

1) How do we get <u>limestone</u> out of the ground?

2) What happens when you <u>heat calcium carbonate</u>?

3) Give the three things you'd get if you added <u>acid</u> to a <u>metal carbonate</u>.

Chemistry 1a — Products from Rocks

Limestone

You've met <u>limestone</u> and <u>calcium oxide</u>. Now it's time to find out about the fab things you can do with the

Calcium Oxide Reacts with Water to Produce Calcium Hydroxide

1) When you <u>add WATER</u> to <u>calcium oxide</u> you get <u>CALCIUM HYDROXIDE</u>.

> calcium oxide + water → calcium hydroxide

- Calcium hydroxide is also called <u>LIMEWATER</u>.
- Limewater can be used to <u>TEST FOR CARBON DIOXIDE</u>.
- The limewater goes <u>CLOUDY</u> if there's carbon dioxide there.

Carbon dioxide

Limewater goes clou

Test for carbon dioxide

2) Calcium hydroxide is an <u>ALKALI</u>.

3) <u>ALKALIS</u> can <u>NEUTRALISE</u> (cancel out) <u>acids</u>.

4) This means calcium hydroxide can <u>neutralise acids</u>.

Limestone is Used to Make Useful Things

Limestone can be used to make <u>CEMENT</u>, <u>MORTAR</u> and <u>CONCRETE</u>.

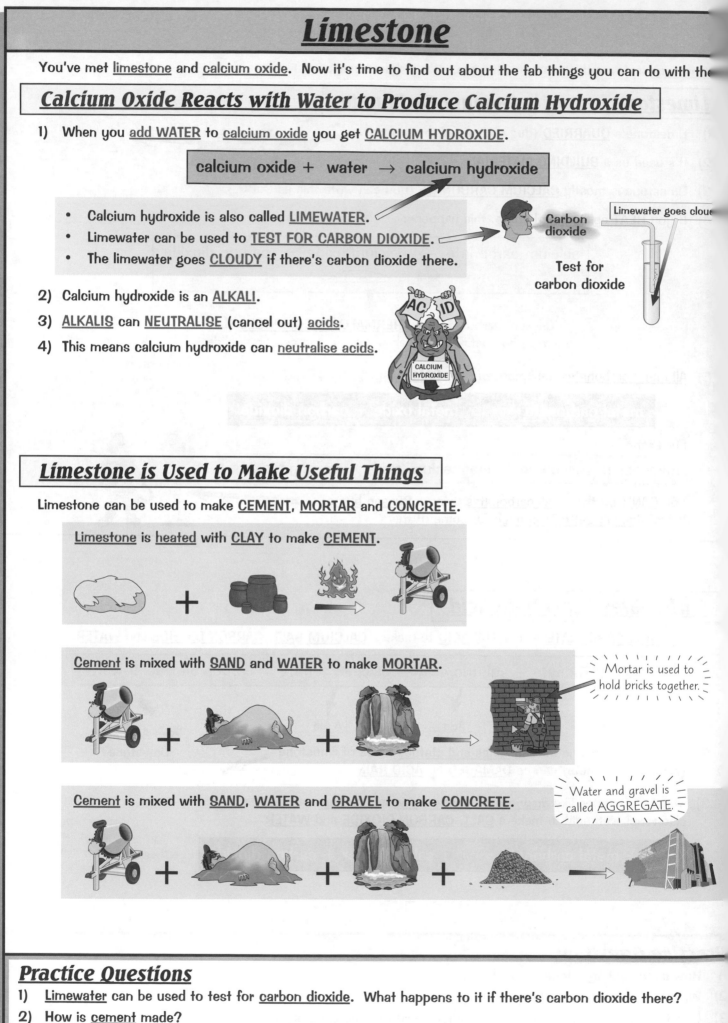

<u>Limestone</u> is <u>heated</u> with <u>CLAY</u> to make <u>CEMENT</u>.

<u>Cement</u> is mixed with <u>SAND</u> and <u>WATER</u> to make <u>MORTAR</u>.

Mortar is used to hold bricks together.

<u>Cement</u> is mixed with <u>SAND</u>, <u>WATER</u> and <u>GRAVEL</u> to make <u>CONCRETE</u>.

Water and gravel is called <u>AGGREGATE</u>.

Practice Questions

1) <u>Limewater</u> can be used to test for <u>carbon dioxide</u>. What happens to it if there's carbon dioxide there?

2) How is <u>cement</u> made?

Using Limestone

Digging limestone out of the ground causes quite a few <u>problems</u>. So does making stuff with it.

Quarrying Limestone Causes Problems

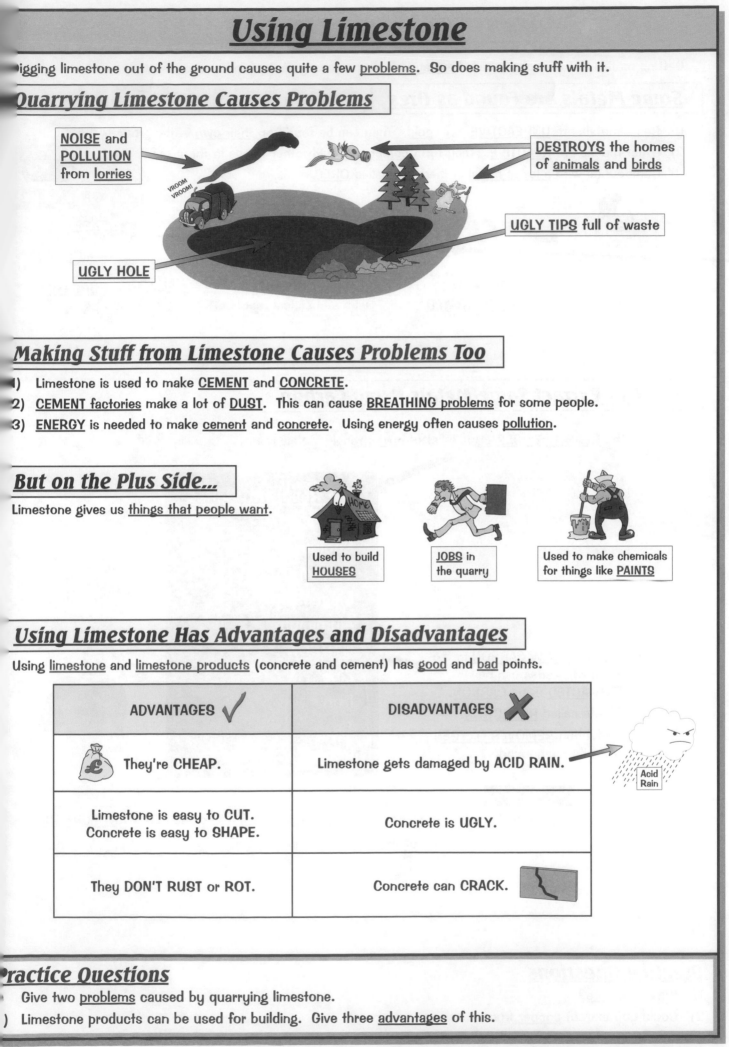

<u>NOISE</u> and <u>POLLUTION</u> from <u>lorries</u>

VROOM! VROOM!

UGLY HOLE

DESTROYS the homes of <u>animals</u> and <u>birds</u>

UGLY TIPS full of waste

Making Stuff from Limestone Causes Problems Too

1) Limestone is used to make <u>CEMENT</u> and <u>CONCRETE</u>.

2) <u>CEMENT</u> <u>factories</u> make a lot of <u>DUST</u>. This can cause <u>BREATHING</u> <u>problems</u> for some people.

3) <u>ENERGY</u> is needed to make <u>cement</u> and <u>concrete</u>. Using energy often causes <u>pollution</u>.

But on the Plus Side...

Limestone gives us <u>things that people want</u>.

Used to build <u>HOUSES</u>

<u>JOBS</u> in the quarry

Used to make chemicals for things like <u>PAINTS</u>

Using Limestone Has Advantages and Disadvantages

Using <u>limestone</u> and <u>limestone products</u> (concrete and cement) has <u>good</u> and <u>bad</u> points.

ADVANTAGES ✓	DISADVANTAGES ✗
They're CHEAP.	Limestone gets damaged by ACID RAIN.
Limestone is easy to CUT. Concrete is easy to SHAPE.	Concrete is UGLY.
They DON'T RUST or ROT.	Concrete can CRACK.

Acid Rain

Practice Questions

1) Give two <u>problems</u> caused by quarrying limestone.

2) Limestone products can be used for building. Give three <u>advantages</u> of this.

Chemistry 1a — Products from Rocks

Getting Metals from Rocks

Getting metals out of rocks is called <u>extraction</u>. Not as scary as it sounds.

Some Metals Are Found as Ores

1) Some metals are <u>UNREACTIVE</u>, e.g. <u>gold</u>. They can be found <u>on their own</u> in the ground.

2) Other metals are <u>REACTIVE</u>. They form <u>compounds</u> with other things in the ground.

3) Compounds with <u>a lot of metal</u> in them are called <u>ORES</u>.

| Metal ore is <u>MINED</u>. | Metal ore is <u>CONCENTRATED</u>. | Metal is <u>EXTRACTED</u> with a chemical reaction. | Metal is <u>PURIFIED</u> (see next page). |

You Can Extract Some Metals Using Carbon

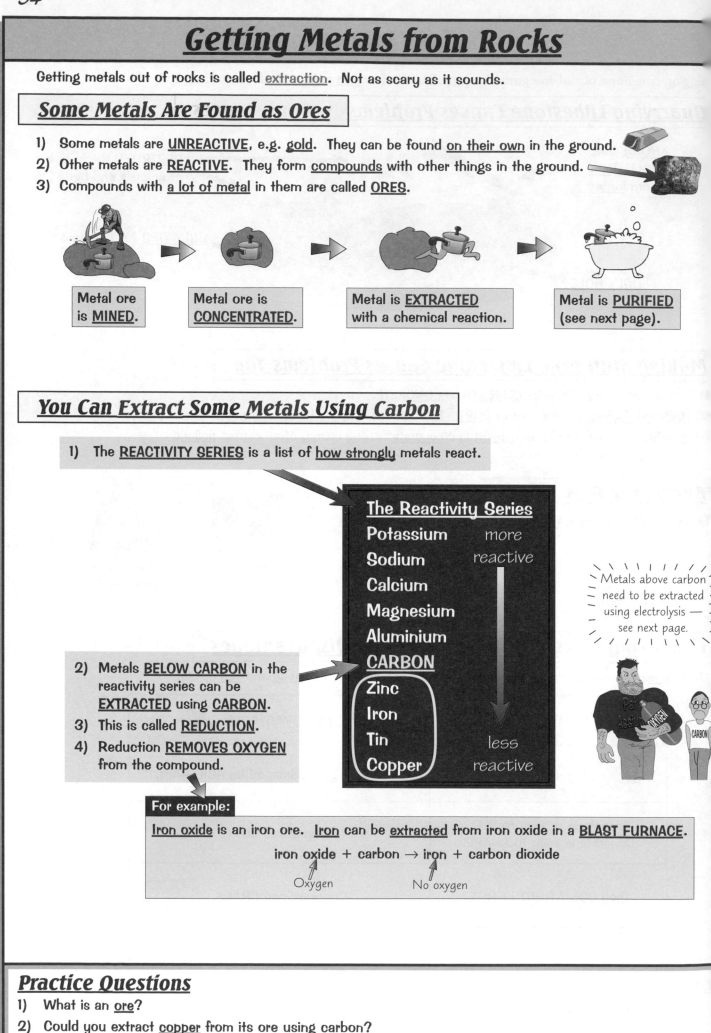

1) The <u>REACTIVITY SERIES</u> is a list of <u>how strongly</u> metals react.

The Reactivity Series

Potassium   more reactive
Sodium
Calcium
Magnesium
Aluminium
<u>CARBON</u>
Zinc
Iron
Tin
Copper   less reactive

Metals above carbon need to be extracted using electrolysis — see next page.

2) Metals <u>BELOW CARBON</u> in the reactivity series can be <u>EXTRACTED</u> using <u>CARBON</u>.

3) This is called <u>REDUCTION</u>.

4) Reduction <u>REMOVES OXYGEN</u> from the compound.

For example:

<u>Iron oxide</u> is an iron ore. <u>Iron</u> can be <u>extracted</u> from iron oxide in a <u>BLAST FURNACE</u>.

iron oxide + carbon → iron + carbon dioxide

Oxygen   No oxygen

Practice Questions

1) What is an <u>ore</u>?

2) Could you extract <u>copper</u> from its ore using carbon?

Getting Metals from Rocks

Electrolysis is used to make metals _purer_. It's also used to _extract_ them from their ores.

Electrolysis Uses Electricity to Break Down Substances

1) Electrolysis is the __BREAKING DOWN__ of a substance using __ELECTRICITY__.

2) When you pass electricity through the substance it breaks down into __POSITIVE IONS__ and __NEGATIVE IONS__.

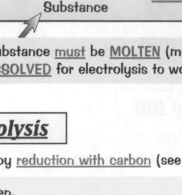

Negative electrode

Positive electrode

3) The __POSITIVE__ ions move towards the __NEGATIVE__ electrode.

4) The __NEGATIVE__ ions move towards the __POSITIVE__ electrode.

Substance

5) The substance _must_ be __MOLTEN__ (melted) or __DISSOLVED__ for electrolysis to work.

Copper is Purified by Electrolysis

Purify means getting rid of any other substances.

1) Copper can be extracted from its ore by reduction with carbon (see page 54).

• Copper ore is __HEATED__ in a big oven.
• This is called __SMELTING__. Smelting __DOESN'T__ give you _totally PURE_ copper.

2) __ELECTROLYSIS__ is used to get __PURE COPPER__.

copper ore + carbon

heat

impure copper

electrolysis

pure copper

Some Metals Have to be Extracted by Electrolysis

1) Some metals are __MORE REACTIVE than carbon__ (e.g. aluminium).

2) They have to be extracted from their ores using __ELECTROLYSIS__.

3) Electrolysis is __EXPENSIVE__. This is because:

• A lot of __ENERGY__ is needed. Energy costs money.
• There are lots of __STAGES__ in the process.

Turn back a page for more about reactivity.

Practice Questions

1) "In electrolysis, negative ions move towards the positive electrode." True or false?

2) Give two uses of electrolysis.

Getting Metals from Rocks

This page has a few more things you need to know about getting hold of copper...

You Can Get Copper From a Solution Using Iron

1) A <u>reactive metal</u> will <u>REPLACE</u> a <u>less reactive metal</u> in a <u>solution</u> of a compound.
2) <u>IRON</u> is <u>more reactive</u> than copper.
3) So <u>scrap IRON</u> can be used to <u>KICK OUT</u> (displace) <u>COPPER</u> from a <u>solution</u> of a <u>copper compound</u>.

A solution is a liquid w
a solid dissolved in it

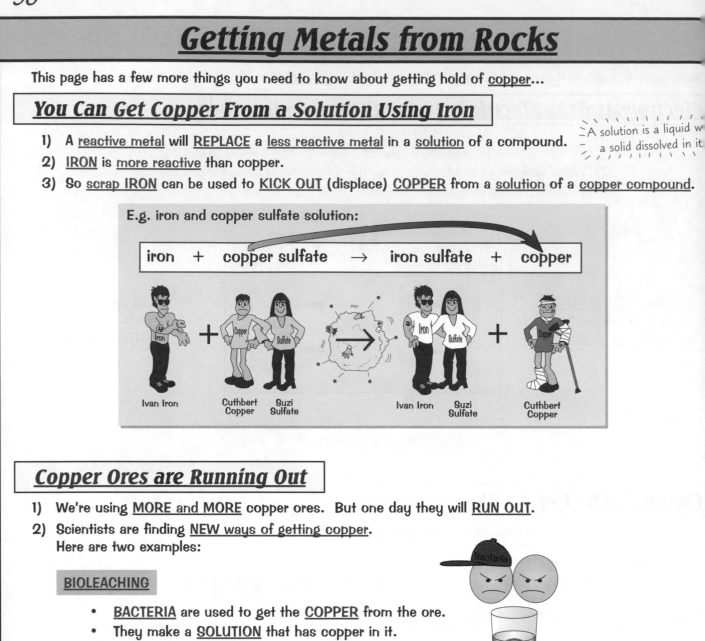

E.g. iron and copper sulfate solution:

iron + copper sulfate → iron sulfate + copper

Ivan Iron Cuthbert Copper Suzi Sulfate Ivan Iron Suzi Sulfate Cuthbert Copper

Copper Ores are Running Out

1) We're using <u>MORE and MORE</u> copper ores. But one day they will <u>RUN OUT</u>.
2) Scientists are finding <u>NEW ways of getting copper</u>. Here are two examples:

BIOLEACHING

- <u>BACTERIA</u> are used to get the <u>COPPER</u> from the ore.
- They make a <u>SOLUTION</u> that has copper in it.
- You can then get the <u>COPPER</u> out of the solution.

PHYTOMINING

'Phyto' just means 'plant'
— so phytomining =
plant mining.

OUCH!

<u>PLANTS</u> are grown in soil that has <u>COPPER</u> in it.

The plants <u>TAKE UP</u> the copper.

The plants are <u>BURNT</u>. You get the copper <u>out</u> of the <u>ash</u>.

3) Bioleaching and phytomining are <u>BETTER for the ENVIRONMENT</u> than mining new copper.

Practice Questions

1) Is iron more <u>reactive</u> than copper?
2) Describe the steps in <u>phytomining</u>.

Impacts of Extracting Metals

Getting metals out of the ground is called <u>mining</u>. It gets us the metals we want, but it comes at a price...

Mining Metals Has Advantages and Disadvantages

Mining has a <u>good side</u> and a <u>bad side</u>. You need to know them <u>both</u>.

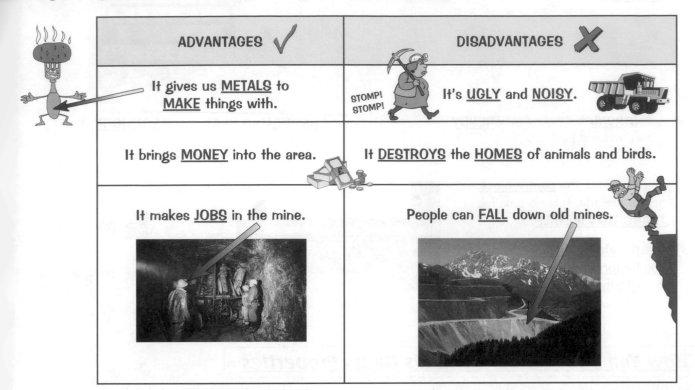

ADVANTAGES ✓	DISADVANTAGES ✗
It gives us <u>METALS</u> to <u>MAKE</u> things with.	STOMP! STOMP! It's <u>UGLY</u> and <u>NOISY</u>.
It brings <u>MONEY</u> into the area.	It <u>DESTROYS</u> the <u>HOMES</u> of animals and birds.
It makes <u>JOBS</u> in the mine.	People can <u>FALL</u> down old mines.

Recycling Metals is Important

1) There's only a <u>set amount</u> of metal in the Earth.
2) To <u>stop it running out</u> we can <u>RECYCLE</u> it (use it again).
3) Here's why recycling is a <u>good idea</u>:

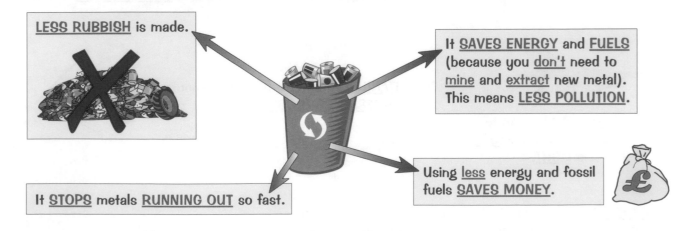

<u>LESS RUBBISH</u> is made.

It <u>SAVES ENERGY</u> and <u>FUELS</u> (because you <u>don't</u> need to <u>mine</u> and <u>extract</u> new metal). This means <u>LESS POLLUTION</u>.

It <u>STOPS</u> metals <u>RUNNING OUT</u> so fast.

Using <u>less</u> energy and fossil fuels <u>SAVES MONEY</u>.

Practice Questions

1) <u>Mining</u> metals has advantages and disadvantages.
   a) Give one <u>advantage</u> of mining for metals.
   b) Give one <u>disadvantage</u> of mining for metals.
2) Give three reasons why <u>recycling</u> metals is important.

Properties of Metals

All metals are the same in some ways. But they're NOT all EXACTLY the same.

Metals are Strong and Bendy and They're Great Conductors

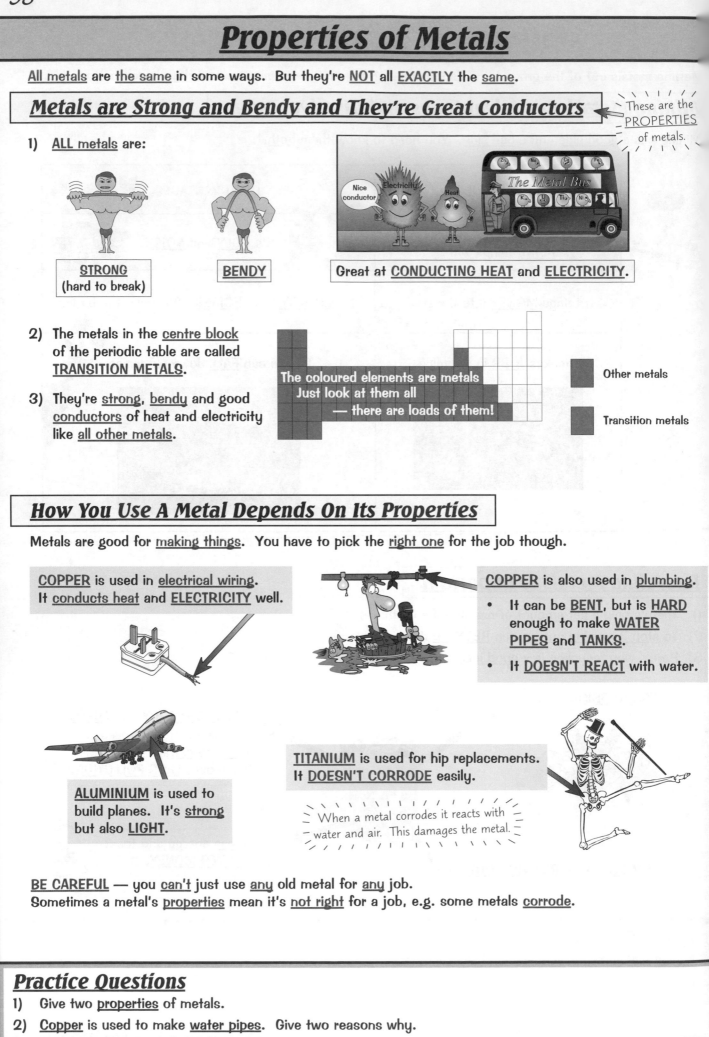

These are the PROPERTIES of metals.

1) ALL metals are:

STRONG (hard to break)

BENDY

Great at CONDUCTING HEAT and ELECTRICITY.

2) The metals in the centre block of the periodic table are called TRANSITION METALS.

3) They're strong, bendy and good conductors of heat and electricity like all other metals.

The coloured elements are metals Just look at them all — there are loads of them!

Other metals

Transition metals

How You Use A Metal Depends On Its Properties

Metals are good for making things. You have to pick the right one for the job though.

COPPER is used in electrical wiring. It conducts heat and ELECTRICITY well.

COPPER is also used in plumbing.

- It can be BENT, but is HARD enough to make WATER PIPES and TANKS.
- It DOESN'T REACT with water.

ALUMINIUM is used to build planes. It's strong but also LIGHT.

TITANIUM is used for hip replacements. It DOESN'T CORRODE easily.

When a metal corrodes it reacts with water and air. This damages the metal.

BE CAREFUL — you can't just use any old metal for any job.
Sometimes a metal's properties mean it's not right for a job, e.g. some metals corrode.

Practice Questions
1) Give two properties of metals.
2) Copper is used to make water pipes. Give two reasons why.

Chemistry 1a — Products from Rocks

Alloys

Metals aren't perfect. They're just not good enough for <u>some jobs</u>. That's where <u>alloys</u> come in.

Iron Can Break Easily

1) Iron made in a <u>blast furnace</u> (see page 54) is only <u>96% iron</u>.
2) It's called <u>CAST IRON</u>.
3) It doesn't have many uses because it's <u>BRITTLE</u> (easy to break).

Most Iron is Turned into Steel — an Alloy

1) An <u>ALLOY</u> is a <u>MIXTURE</u> of two or more <u>metals</u>. Or it can be a <u>MIXTURE</u> of a <u>metal</u> and a <u>non-metal</u>.
2) Most iron is changed into <u>useful alloys</u> called <u>STEELS</u>.
3) <u>Steels</u> are mixtures of <u>IRON</u> and <u>CARBON</u>. Sometimes <u>OTHER METALS</u> are added too.

TYPE OF STEEL	PROPERTY	USE
<u>LOW CARBON STEEL</u>	EASILY SHAPED	CARS
<u>HIGH CARBON STEEL</u>	HARD	BRIDGES
<u>STAINLESS STEEL</u>	DOESN'T CORRODE	KNIVES AND FORKS

Remember, this is when it gets damaged by water and air.

Alloys are Harder Than Pure Metals

1) Pure <u>copper</u>, <u>gold</u>, <u>iron</u> and <u>aluminium</u> are all <u>TOO SOFT</u> for most uses.
2) These metals can be <u>MIXED</u> with <u>other metals</u> to make <u>alloys</u>.
3) <u>ALLOYS</u> of iron and gold are <u>useful</u> because they are <u>HARDER</u> than the pure metals.

Gold $+$ Other metal $\rightarrow$ Alloy

4) We can <u>make</u> alloys that are right for the <u>jobs</u> we need them for.
5) <u>Many metals</u> you see everyday are <u>alloys</u>.

Practice Questions

1) Why does <u>cast iron</u> not have many uses?
2) What is an <u>alloy</u>?

Using Crude Oil as a Fuel

Crude oil is super useful. But it's too good to be true — it has some <u>problems</u>.

Crude Oil Gives Us Fuels

<u>EXTRACTING</u> (getting) crude oil is a <u>BIG INDUSTRY</u>.	Crude oil <u>FRACTIONS</u> make good <u>FUELS</u>.	<u>FUELS</u> give us energy for loads of things like <u>TRANSPORT</u> and <u>HEAT</u>.

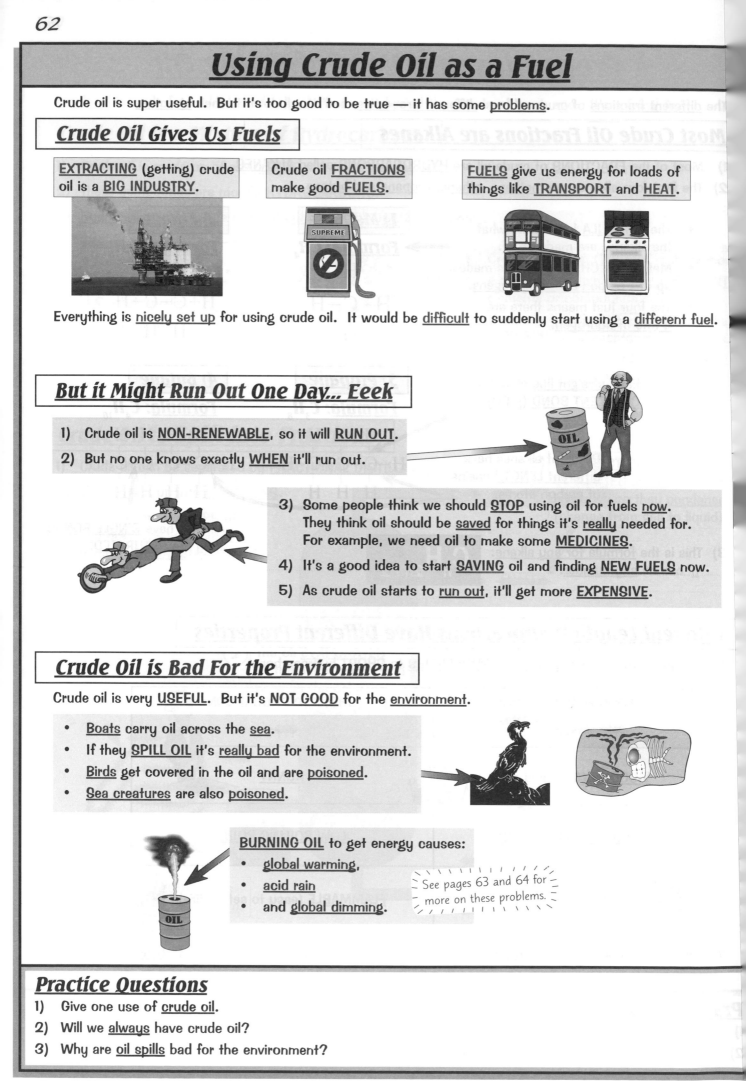

Everything is <u>nicely set up</u> for using crude oil. It would be <u>difficult</u> to suddenly start using a <u>different fuel</u>.

But it Might Run Out One Day... Eeek

1) Crude oil is <u>NON-RENEWABLE</u>, so it will <u>RUN OUT</u>.

2) But no one knows exactly <u>WHEN</u> it'll run out.

3) Some people think we should <u>STOP</u> using oil for fuels <u>now</u>. They think oil should be <u>saved</u> for things it's <u>really</u> needed for. For example, we need oil to make some <u>MEDICINES</u>.

4) It's a good idea to start <u>SAVING</u> oil and finding <u>NEW FUELS</u> now.

5) As crude oil starts to <u>run out</u>, it'll get more <u>EXPENSIVE</u>.

Crude Oil is Bad For the Environment

Crude oil is very <u>USEFUL</u>. But it's <u>NOT GOOD</u> for the <u>environment</u>.

- <u>Boats</u> carry oil across the <u>sea</u>.
- If they <u>SPILL OIL</u> it's <u>really bad</u> for the environment.
- <u>Birds</u> get covered in the oil and are <u>poisoned</u>.
- <u>Sea creatures</u> are also <u>poisoned</u>.

<u>BURNING OIL</u> to get energy causes:
- <u>global warming</u>,
- <u>acid rain</u>
- and <u>global dimming</u>.

See pages 63 and 64 for more on these problems.

Practice Questions

1) Give one use of <u>crude oil</u>.

2) Will we <u>always</u> have crude oil?

3) Why are <u>oil spills</u> bad for the environment?

Environmental Problems

We <u>burn fuels</u> all the time to make energy.

Burning Fossil Fuels Gives Off Gases and Particles

1) <u>Burning fuels</u> is called <u>COMBUSTION</u>.
2) <u>HEAT</u> is given off when you burn <u>HYDROCARBON FUELS</u> (made up of carbon and hydrogen).
3) <u>SOLID PARTICLES</u> can also be given off. These can be <u>SOOT</u>.
   They can also be <u>fuel that HASN'T BURNT</u>.

Particles are just little bits of solid.

4) When a fuel burns these <u>GASES</u> are also given off:

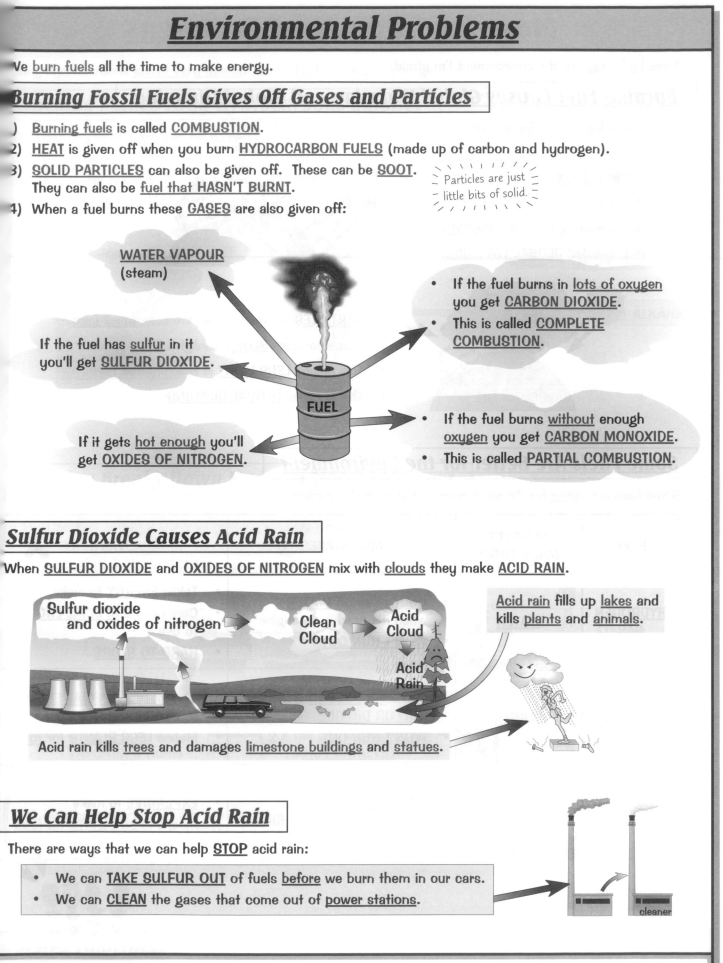

<u>WATER VAPOUR</u>
(steam)

If the fuel has <u>sulfur</u> in it you'll get <u>SULFUR DIOXIDE</u>.

If it gets <u>hot enough</u> you'll get <u>OXIDES OF NITROGEN</u>.

FUEL

- If the fuel burns in <u>lots of oxygen</u> you get <u>CARBON DIOXIDE</u>.
- This is called <u>COMPLETE COMBUSTION</u>.

- If the fuel burns <u>without</u> enough <u>oxygen</u> you get <u>CARBON MONOXIDE</u>.
- This is called <u>PARTIAL COMBUSTION</u>.

Sulfur Dioxide Causes Acid Rain

When <u>SULFUR DIOXIDE</u> and <u>OXIDES OF NITROGEN</u> mix with <u>clouds</u> they make <u>ACID RAIN</u>.

Sulfur dioxide and oxides of nitrogen

Clean Cloud

Acid Cloud

Acid Rain

<u>Acid rain</u> fills up <u>lakes</u> and kills <u>plants</u> and <u>animals</u>.

Acid rain kills <u>trees</u> and damages <u>limestone buildings</u> and <u>statues</u>.

We Can Help Stop Acid Rain

There are ways that we can help <u>STOP</u> acid rain:

- We can <u>TAKE SULFUR OUT</u> of fuels <u>before</u> we burn them in our cars.
- We can <u>CLEAN</u> the gases that come out of <u>power stations</u>.

cleaner

Practice Questions

1) List two gases that are given off when a <u>hydrocarbon fuel</u> is burnt.
2) Give two gases that cause <u>acid rain</u>.

Alkenes and Ethanol

You get <u>alkenes</u> from cracking long hydrocarbons (see page 65).

> Don't get alkenes muddled up with alkanes. They were on page 61.

Alkenes Have a Carbon=Carbon Double Bond

1) Alkenes are <u>HYDROCARBONS</u>.
2) The first two alkenes are <u>ethene</u> and <u>propene</u>.

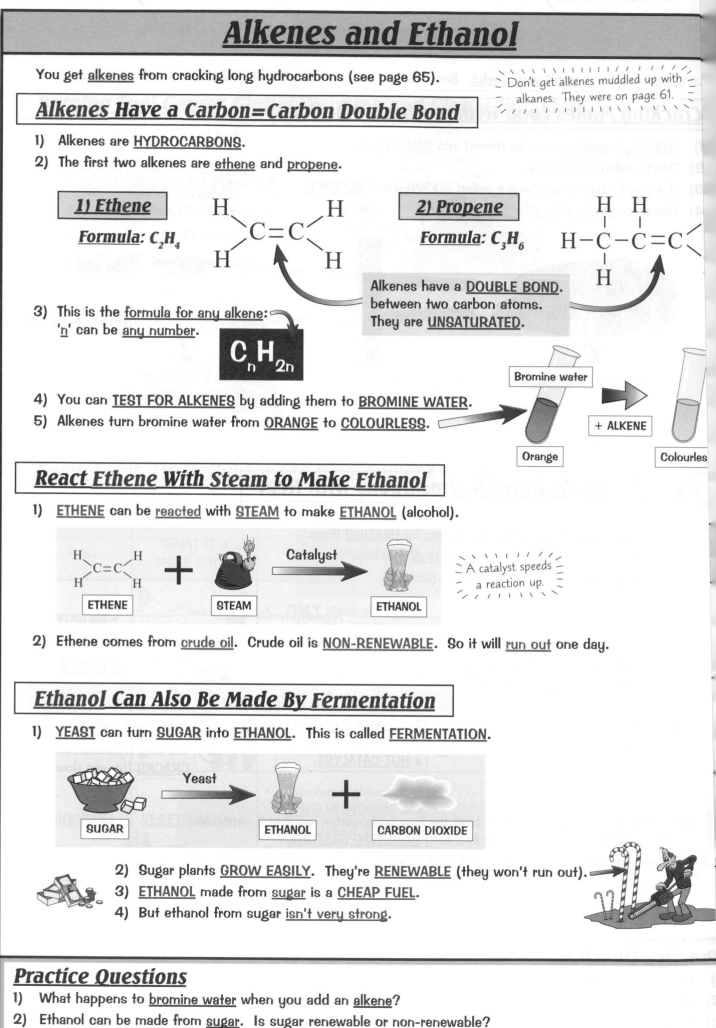

1) Ethene
<u>Formula</u>: C_2H_4

2) Propene
<u>Formula</u>: C_3H_6

Alkenes have a <u>DOUBLE BOND</u>. between two carbon atoms. They are <u>UNSATURATED</u>.

3) This is the <u>formula for any alkene</u>: '<u>n</u>' can be <u>any number</u>.

$$C_nH_{2n}$$

4) You can <u>TEST FOR ALKENES</u> by adding them to <u>BROMINE WATER</u>.
5) Alkenes turn bromine water from <u>ORANGE</u> to <u>COLOURLESS</u>.

Bromine water

+ ALKENE

Orange

Colourles

React Ethene With Steam to Make Ethanol

1) <u>ETHENE</u> can be <u>reacted</u> with <u>STEAM</u> to make <u>ETHANOL</u> (alcohol).

ETHENE   +   STEAM   Catalyst →   ETHANOL

> A catalyst speeds a reaction up.

2) Ethene comes from <u>crude oil</u>. Crude oil is <u>NON-RENEWABLE</u>. So it will <u>run out</u> one day.

Ethanol Can Also Be Made By Fermentation

1) <u>YEAST</u> can turn <u>SUGAR</u> into <u>ETHANOL</u>. This is called <u>FERMENTATION</u>.

SUGAR   Yeast →   ETHANOL   +   CARBON DIOXIDE

2) Sugar plants <u>GROW EASILY</u>. They're <u>RENEWABLE</u> (they won't run out).
3) <u>ETHANOL</u> made from <u>sugar</u> is a <u>CHEAP FUEL</u>.
4) But ethanol from sugar <u>isn't very strong</u>.

Practice Questions

1) What happens to <u>bromine water</u> when you add an <u>alkene</u>?
2) Ethanol can be made from <u>sugar</u>. Is sugar renewable or non-renewable?

Using Alkenes to Make Polymers

Polymers are just about everywhere you look. We can make them from alkenes.

Alkenes Can Be Used to Make Polymers

1) Small molecules are called MONOMERS.
2) These can join together to make very long molecules called POLYMERS.
3) Lots of SMALL ALKENE MOLECULES (monomers) join to form VERY LARGE MOLECULES (polymers).

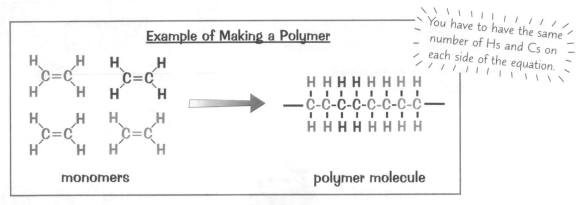

You have to have the same number of Hs and Cs on each side of the equation.

Example of Making a Polymer

monomers → polymer molecule

4) Lots of ETHENE molecules join together to make POLY(ETHENE).
5) Lots of PROPENE molecules join together to make POLY(PROPENE).

Polymers Have Lots of Different Uses

Polymers are REALLY USEFUL. Scientists come up with NEW USES all the time. Here are some:

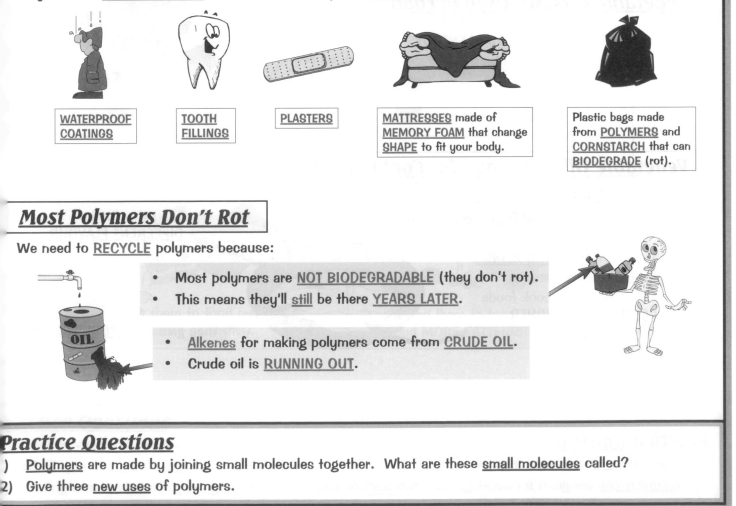

WATERPROOF COATINGS

TOOTH FILLINGS

PLASTERS

MATTRESSES made of MEMORY FOAM that change SHAPE to fit your body.

Plastic bags made from POLYMERS and CORNSTARCH that can BIODEGRADE (rot).

Most Polymers Don't Rot

We need to RECYCLE polymers because:

- Most polymers are NOT BIODEGRADABLE (they don't rot).
- This means they'll still be there YEARS LATER.

- Alkenes for making polymers come from CRUDE OIL.
- Crude oil is RUNNING OUT.

Practice Questions

1) Polymers are made by joining small molecules together. What are these small molecules called?
2) Give three new uses of polymers.

Emulsions

Emulsions are found in <u>foods</u>, <u>cosmetics</u> and <u>paint</u>. And in exams...

Emulsions Can Be Made from Oil and Water

1) Oils <u>DON'T DISSOLVE IN WATER</u>.

2) You can <u>SHAKE</u> oil and water together to make them <u>mix</u>. This makes an <u>EMULSION</u>.

3) Emulsions are made up of lots of <u>DROPLETS</u> of <u>one liquid</u> in <u>another liquid</u>.

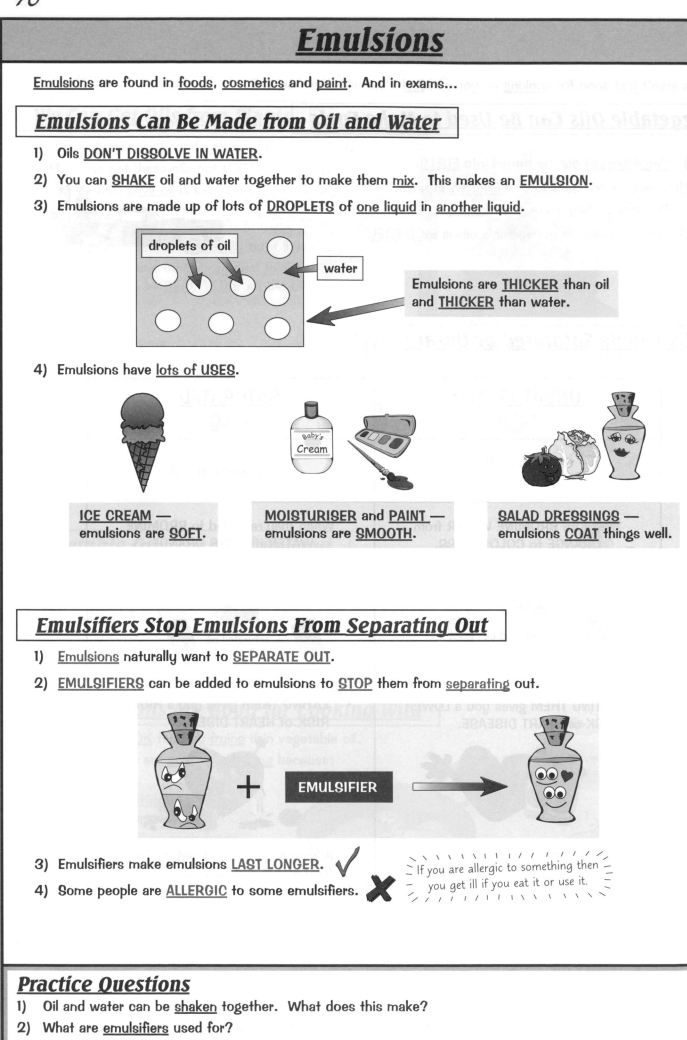

droplets of oil

water

Emulsions are <u>THICKER</u> than oil and <u>THICKER</u> than water.

4) Emulsions have <u>lots of USES</u>.

<u>ICE CREAM</u> — emulsions are <u>SOFT</u>.

Baby's Cream

<u>MOISTURISER</u> and <u>PAINT</u> — emulsions are <u>SMOOTH</u>.

<u>SALAD DRESSINGS</u> — emulsions <u>COAT</u> things well.

Emulsifiers Stop Emulsions From Separating Out

1) <u>Emulsions</u> naturally want to <u>SEPARATE OUT</u>.

2) <u>EMULSIFIERS</u> can be added to emulsions to <u>STOP</u> them from <u>separating</u> out.

+ EMULSIFIER →

3) Emulsifiers make emulsions <u>LAST LONGER</u>. ✓

4) Some people are <u>ALLERGIC</u> to some emulsifiers. ✗

If you are allergic to something then you get ill if you eat it or use it.

Practice Questions

1) Oil and water can be <u>shaken</u> together. What does this make?

2) What are <u>emulsifiers</u> used for?

Continental Drift

People used to think they knew why the Earth is all <u>crinkly</u>. Then <u>Wegener</u> came along with a new idea...

Wegener's Theory of Continental Drift...

1) Scientists used to think that the Earth <u>SHRUNK</u> and <u>CRINKLED</u> as it <u>COOLED DOWN</u>. They thought that this made <u>MOUNTAINS</u>.

2) A man called <u>WEGENER</u> had a <u>different idea</u>. He called his idea <u>CONTINENTAL DRIFT</u>.

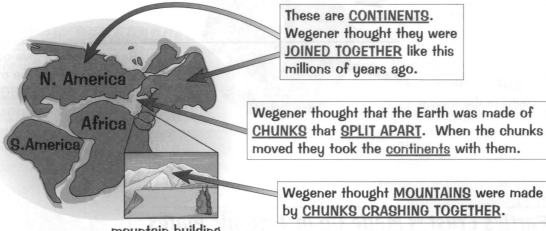

These are <u>CONTINENTS</u>. Wegener thought they were <u>JOINED TOGETHER</u> like this millions of years ago.

Wegener thought that the Earth was made of <u>CHUNKS</u> that <u>SPLIT APART</u>. When the chunks moved they took the <u>continents</u> with them.

Wegener thought <u>MOUNTAINS</u> were made by <u>CHUNKS CRASHING TOGETHER</u>.

mountain building

Why Wegener had his idea:

- Wegener had seen that the <u>continents</u> would fit together like a <u>JIGSAW</u>.
- He also found <u>MATCHING FOSSILS</u> in <u>different continents</u>.
- There were <u>MATCHING PATTERNS</u> in the <u>ROCKS</u> in different continents too.

Nobody Believed Wegener For a Long Time

Most scientists <u>DIDN'T BELIEVE</u> Wegener's theory. Here's why...

1) Wegener <u>didn't</u> have much <u>EVIDENCE</u> that he was right.

2) This meant that he <u>couldn't</u> really <u>EXPLAIN</u> his idea.

3) Most people thought the continents <u>used to be joined together</u> by <u>LAND BRIDGES</u>.

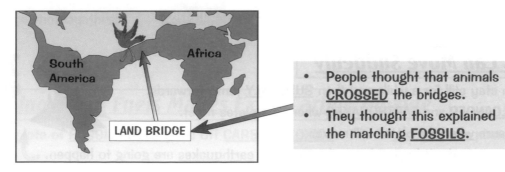

- People thought that animals <u>CROSSED</u> the bridges.
- They thought this explained the matching <u>FOSSILS</u>.

4) In the end, <u>NEW EVIDENCE</u> showed that Wegener was <u>RIGHT</u> all along.

Practice Questions

1) "Wegener thought that the Earth was made of <u>chunks</u> that <u>split apart</u>." True or false?

2) Give one reason why people <u>didn't believe</u> Wegener's theory at first.

Chemistry 1b — Oils, Earth and Atmosphere

Infrared Radiation

Heat energy can be transferred (moved) from one place to another.

Infrared Radiation is Heat

1) INFRARED RADIATION is just a fancy name for the heat given out by objects (things).

2) All objects EMIT (give out) and ABSORB (take in) infrared radiation.

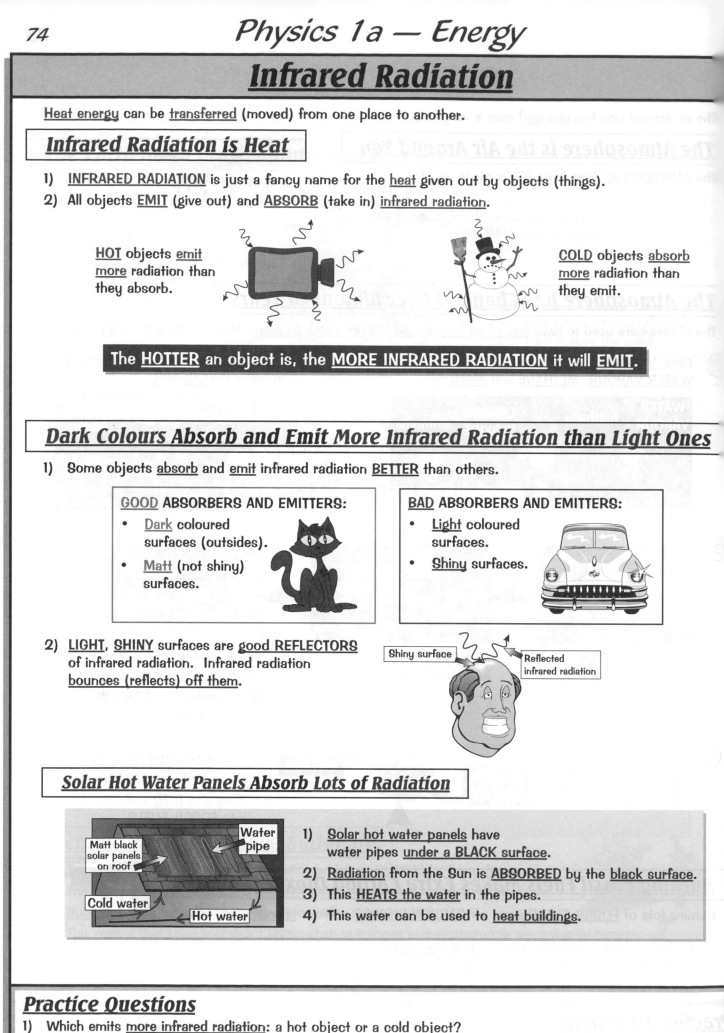

HOT objects emit more radiation than they absorb.

COLD objects absorb more radiation than they emit.

The HOTTER an object is, the MORE INFRARED RADIATION it will EMIT.

Dark Colours Absorb and Emit More Infrared Radiation than Light Ones

1) Some objects absorb and emit infrared radiation BETTER than others.

GOOD ABSORBERS AND EMITTERS:
- Dark coloured surfaces (outsides).
- Matt (not shiny) surfaces.

BAD ABSORBERS AND EMITTERS:
- Light coloured surfaces.
- Shiny surfaces.

2) LIGHT, SHINY surfaces are good REFLECTORS of infrared radiation. Infrared radiation bounces (reflects) off them.

Shiny surface

Reflected infrared radiation

Solar Hot Water Panels Absorb Lots of Radiation

Matt black solar panels on roof

Water pipe

Cold water

Hot water

1) Solar hot water panels have water pipes under a BLACK surface.

2) Radiation from the Sun is ABSORBED by the black surface.

3) This HEATS the water in the pipes.

4) This water can be used to heat buildings.

Practice Questions

1) Which emits more infrared radiation: a hot object or a cold object?

2) True or false: a dark coloured object will be a good absorber of infrared radiation.

3) What colour are solar hot water panels?

Solids, Liquids and Gases

Solids and liquids and gases, oh my.

Solids, Liquids and Gases are all Made up of Particles

1) <u>MATTER</u> is just a name for the stuff <u>everything</u> is made from.

2) Matter is either a <u>SOLID</u>, a <u>LIQUID</u> or a <u>GAS</u>.

3) All matter is made up of tiny <u>PARTICLES</u> — you can just think of them as <u>tiny balls</u>.

4) The way the particles are <u>ARRANGED</u> is <u>different</u> in solids, liquids and gases.

5) The <u>ENERGY</u> of the particles is <u>different</u> too.

particles

Solids

1) The particles in a <u>solid</u> are <u>very CLOSE TOGETHER</u> like this.

2) The particles make a set <u>pattern</u>.

3) The particles <u>don't</u> have much <u>energy</u>.

4) They <u>can't move</u> very much — they can only vibrate (jiggle about a bit).

Liquids

1) The particles in a <u>liquid</u> are <u>quite close together</u>.

2) The particles <u>DON'T</u> make a set <u>pattern</u>.

3) The particles have <u>more energy</u> than particles in a <u>solid</u>.

4) They can <u>move</u> past each other.

5) They move <u>faster</u> than the particles in a <u>solid</u>.

Gases

1) The particles in a <u>gas</u> are <u>FAR APART</u> and <u>NOT</u> in a pattern.

2) The particles have <u>a lot</u> of energy.

3) They have <u>more energy</u> than particles in a <u>liquid</u>.

4) They move <u>really quickly</u>.

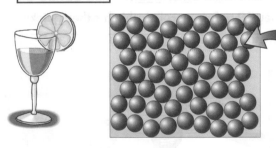
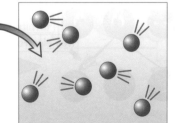

Practice Questions

1) True or false: the particles in a <u>solid</u> are in a pattern.

2) True or false: particles in a <u>gas</u> have <u>less energy</u> than particles in a <u>liquid</u>.

Condensation and Evaporation

Want another super fun page on <u>gases</u> and <u>liquids</u>? You're in luck...

Evaporation is when a Liquid Changes into a Gas

1) The particles in a <u>liquid</u> can <u>escape</u> to form a <u>gas</u>.
This is called <u>EVAPORATION</u>.

2) Particles can only escape if:

- They are <u>near the surface</u> of the liquid.
- They are travelling in the <u>right direction</u>.
- They have <u>enough energy</u> to escape the liquid.

3) Only particles with <u>low energies</u> are left in
the liquid. So the liquid <u>cools down</u>.

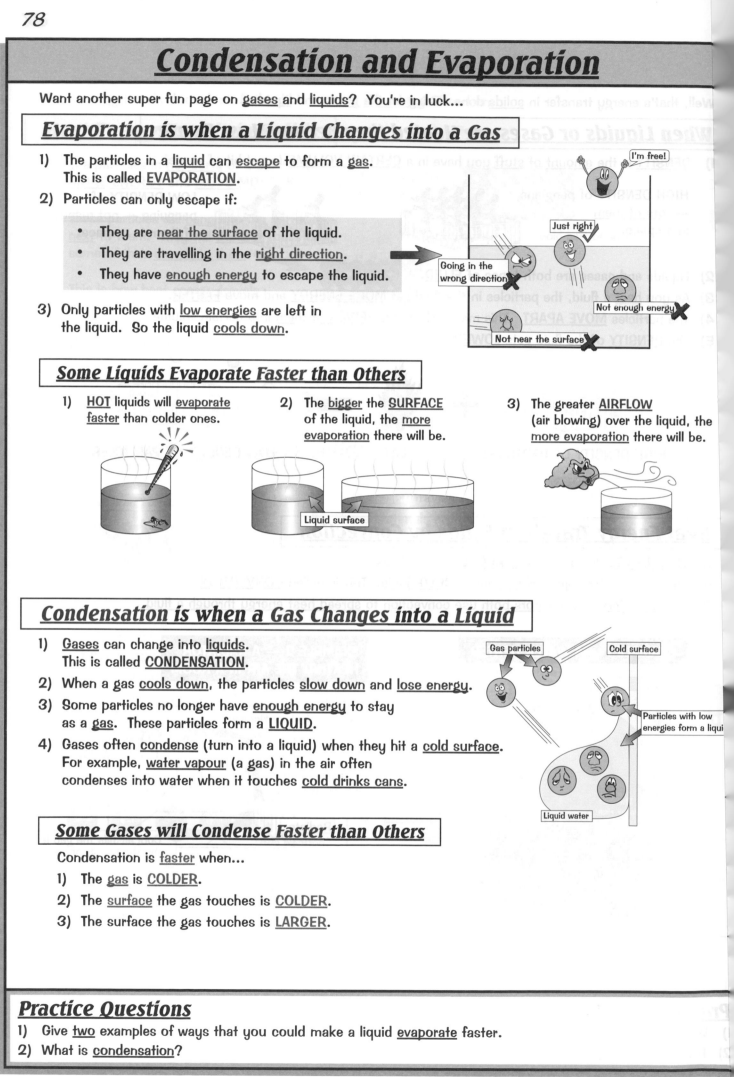

I'm free!

Just right ✓

Going in the
wrong direction ✗

Not enough energy ✗

Not near the surface ✗

Some Liquids Evaporate Faster than Others

1) <u>HOT</u> liquids will <u>evaporate</u>
<u>faster</u> than colder ones.

2) The <u>bigger</u> the <u>SURFACE</u>
of the liquid, the <u>more</u>
<u>evaporation</u> there will be.

Liquid surface

3) The greater <u>AIRFLOW</u>
(air blowing) over the liquid, the
<u>more evaporation</u> there will be.

Condensation is when a Gas Changes into a Liquid

1) <u>Gases</u> can change into <u>liquids</u>.
This is called <u>CONDENSATION</u>.

2) When a gas <u>cools down</u>, the particles <u>slow down</u> and <u>lose energy</u>.

3) Some particles no longer have <u>enough energy</u> to stay
as a <u>gas</u>. These particles form a <u>LIQUID</u>.

4) Gases often <u>condense</u> (turn into a liquid) when they hit a <u>cold surface</u>.
For example, <u>water vapour</u> (a gas) in the air often
condenses into water when it touches <u>cold drinks cans</u>.

Gas particles

Cold surface

Particles with low
energies form a liqui

Liquid water

Some Gases will Condense Faster than Others

Condensation is <u>faster</u> when...

1) The <u>gas</u> is <u>COLDER</u>.

2) The <u>surface</u> the gas touches is <u>COLDER</u>.

3) The surface the gas touches is <u>LARGER</u>.

Practice Questions

1) Give <u>two</u> examples of ways that you could make a liquid <u>evaporate</u> faster.

2) What is <u>condensation</u>?

Rate of Heat Transfer

Sorry folks, it's another rocking page about heat energy...

Different Objects give out Different Amounts of Heat Energy

1) The rate of heat transfer is how much heat energy is transferred (passed on) in a certain time.

2) The rate an object transfers energy depends on many things...

SURFACE AREA

1) The amount of surface an object has is called its surface area.

2) The **BIGGER** the **SURFACE AREA** of an object, the **HIGHER** the rate of heat transfer. (It will give out more heat in a given time.)

Large surface area, lots of heat given out.

Small surface area, less heat given out.

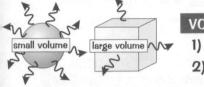

small volume   large volume

The smaller the volume, the higher the rate of heat transfer.

VOLUME

1) The volume of an object is the amount of space it takes up.

2) The smaller the volume of the object, the higher the rate of heat transfer. (As long as its surface area and start temperature are the same.)

THE MATERIAL THE OBJECT IS MADE FROM

Objects made from **CONDUCTORS** (see p. 76) have a higher rate of heat transfer than **INSULATORS**. They transfer energy faster.

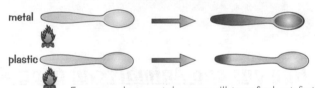

metal

plastic

For example, a metal spoon will transfer heat faster than a spoon made from an insulator like plastic.

THE MATERIAL THE OBJECT IS TOUCHING

An object will transfer energy faster if it is touching a **CONDUCTOR**.

For example, metal is a good conductor. A metal spoon will conduct heat away from a hot drink more quickly than a plastic spoon.

metal   plastic

THE TEMPERATURE DIFFERENCE

The **BIGGER** the temperature difference between an object and its surroundings, the **FASTER** heat energy is transferred.

Some Objects are Made to Transfer Heat Quickly

1) Some objects are designed (made) to transfer heat quickly.

2) These objects have a high rate of heat transfer.

3) They are usually made of conductors like metal.

4) They have a large surface area.

For example, the cooling fins on an engine are made from metal and have a large surface area. They transfer heat quickly. This stops the engine from getting too hot.

Practice Questions

1) True or false: conductors transfer heat faster than insulators.

2) Why do cooling fins have a big surface area?

Rate of Heat Transfer

Some things are specially made to <u>reduce</u> the rate of heat transfer.

Vacuum Flasks are Designed to Reduce Heat Transfer

<u>Vacuum flasks</u> help <u>stop heat being lost</u> from the liquid inside them.
That's how they keep your <u>tea</u> nice and <u>hot</u>.

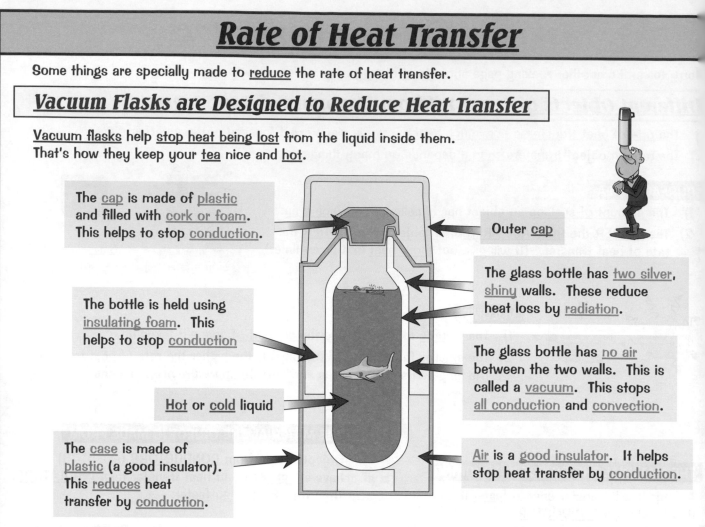

The <u>cap</u> is made of <u>plastic</u> and filled with <u>cork or foam</u>. This helps to stop <u>conduction</u>.

Outer <u>cap</u>

The glass bottle has <u>two silver</u>, <u>shiny</u> walls. These reduce heat loss by <u>radiation</u>.

The bottle is held using <u>insulating foam</u>. This helps to stop <u>conduction</u>

The glass bottle has <u>no air</u> between the two walls. This is called a <u>vacuum</u>. This stops <u>all conduction</u> and <u>convection</u>.

<u>Hot</u> or <u>cold</u> liquid

The <u>case</u> is made of <u>plastic</u> (a good insulator). This <u>reduces</u> heat transfer by <u>conduction</u>.

<u>Air</u> is a <u>good insulator</u>. It helps stop heat transfer by <u>conduction</u>.

Humans and Animals can Control Heat Transfer

TRAPPING AIR HELPS KEEP YOU WARM

1) <u>Air</u> is an <u>INSULATOR</u>.
2) When humans and animals get cold, the hairs on their bodies 'stand up'. This <u>traps</u> a <u>layer of air</u> around them.
3) Humans also use <u>CLOTHES</u> to keep themselves warm. These also <u>trap air</u>.
4) Trapping a layer of air helps to stop heat loss by <u>CONDUCTION</u> and <u>CONVECTION</u>.

HAVING A LARGE SURFACE AREA HELPS KEEP YOU COOL

For example, animals that live in <u>hot places</u> have <u>huge ears</u>. These have a <u>large surface area</u>. This helps them <u>lose a lot of heat</u> by <u>radiation</u> and keep cool.

Animals that live in <u>cold places</u> have <u>small ears</u>. These have a <u>small surface area</u>. This helps to reduce <u>heat loss</u> by <u>radiation</u>.

Practice Questions
1) What is a <u>vacuum flask</u> designed to do?
2) Why do animals that live in hot places have <u>large ears</u>?

Energy Efficiency in the Home

There are lots of things you can do to stop <u>heat energy</u> being <u>lost</u> from a building.

Insulation Reduces Heat Loss from Homes

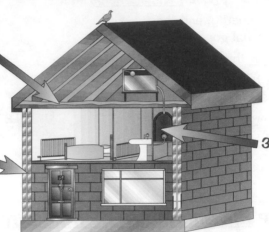

1) <u>LOFT INSULATION</u> is a thick layer of fibreglass wool. It reduces <u>conduction</u> and <u>radiation</u> of heat energy through the ceiling.

2) There is usually a <u>gap</u> between the bricks in walls. <u>Foam</u> can be squirted into this gap. This is called <u>CAVITY WALL INSULATION</u>.

The gap reduces <u>conduction</u>. The foam traps pockets of air to reduce <u>convection</u>.

3) <u>HOT WATER TANK JACKET</u> This is a cover made from an insulator. It reduces <u>conduction</u> and <u>radiation</u>.

U-Values Tell You How Well Heat can Travel through a Material

1) Materials have different <u>U-values</u>.

2) The <u>lower</u> the U-value, the <u>better</u> the material is at being an <u>insulator</u>.

Heat energy → High U-Value → Heat energy

<u>Lots</u> of heat energy passes through the material. It's a <u>conductor</u>.

Heat energy → Low U-Value → Heat energy

<u>Not much</u> heat energy passes through the material. It's an <u>insulator</u>.

You can Save Money on Heating by using Insulation

1) <u>Buying insulation</u> for your home <u>costs money</u>. But it can <u>save</u> you money on heating bills.

2) Over time, the <u>money you save</u> on heating bills <u>equals</u> the <u>money you spent</u> on buying the insulation.

3) The <u>time</u> it takes to save the amount of money you spent is called the <u>PAYBACK TIME</u>.

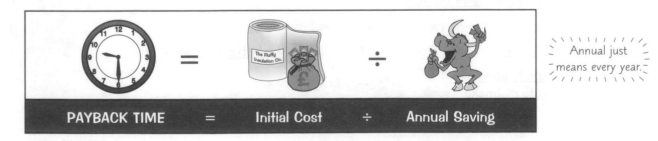

| PAYBACK TIME | = | Initial Cost | ÷ | Annual Saving |

Annual just means every year.

4) The <u>more money</u> you save <u>over a period of time</u>, the more <u>COST EFFECTIVE</u> the insulation is.

Practice Questions

1) Why are houses fitted with <u>insulation</u>?

2) What is <u>payback time</u>?

Specific Heat Capacity

Specific heat capacity sounds a bit scary — but it's not that bad, so read on...

Specific Heat Capacity Tells You How Much Energy Stuff Can Store

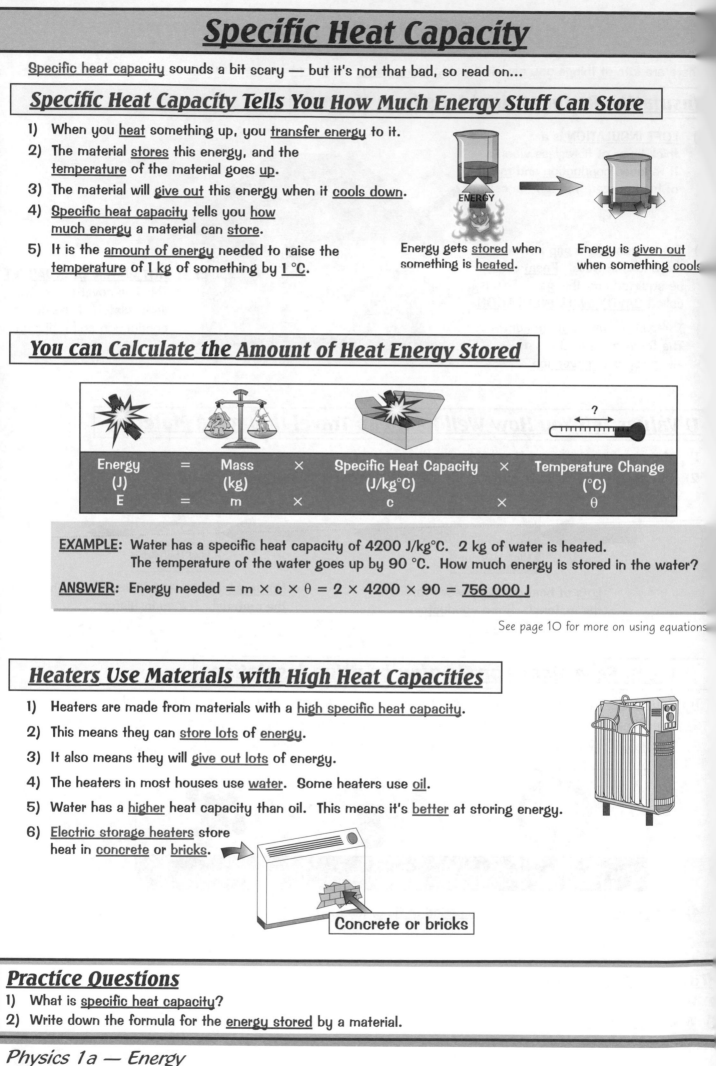

1) When you <u>heat</u> something up, you <u>transfer energy</u> to it.

2) The material <u>stores</u> this energy, and the <u>temperature</u> of the material goes <u>up</u>.

3) The material will <u>give out</u> this energy when it <u>cools down</u>.

4) <u>Specific heat capacity</u> tells you <u>how much energy</u> a material can <u>store</u>.

5) It is the <u>amount of energy</u> needed to raise the <u>temperature</u> of <u>1 kg</u> of something by <u>1 °C</u>.

Energy gets <u>stored</u> when something is <u>heated</u>.

Energy is <u>given out</u> when something cools

You can Calculate the Amount of Heat Energy Stored

Energy (J)	=	Mass (kg)	×	Specific Heat Capacity (J/kg°C)	×	Temperature Change (°C)
E	=	m	×	c	×	θ

<u>EXAMPLE</u>: Water has a specific heat capacity of 4200 J/kg°C. 2 kg of water is heated. The temperature of the water goes up by 90 °C. How much energy is stored in the water?

<u>ANSWER</u>: Energy needed = m × c × θ = 2 × 4200 × 90 = <u>756 000 J</u>

See page 10 for more on using equations

Heaters Use Materials with High Heat Capacities

1) Heaters are made from materials with a <u>high specific heat capacity</u>.

2) This means they can <u>store lots</u> of <u>energy</u>.

3) It also means they will <u>give out lots</u> of energy.

4) The heaters in most houses use <u>water</u>. Some heaters use <u>oil</u>.

5) Water has a <u>higher</u> heat capacity than oil. This means it's <u>better</u> at storing energy.

6) <u>Electric storage heaters</u> store heat in <u>concrete</u> or <u>bricks</u>.

Concrete or bricks

Practice Questions

1) What is <u>specific heat capacity</u>?

2) Write down the formula for the <u>energy stored</u> by a material.

Energy Transfer

Heat is just one type of energy. Energy comes in lots of different types...

Learn These Nine Types of Energy

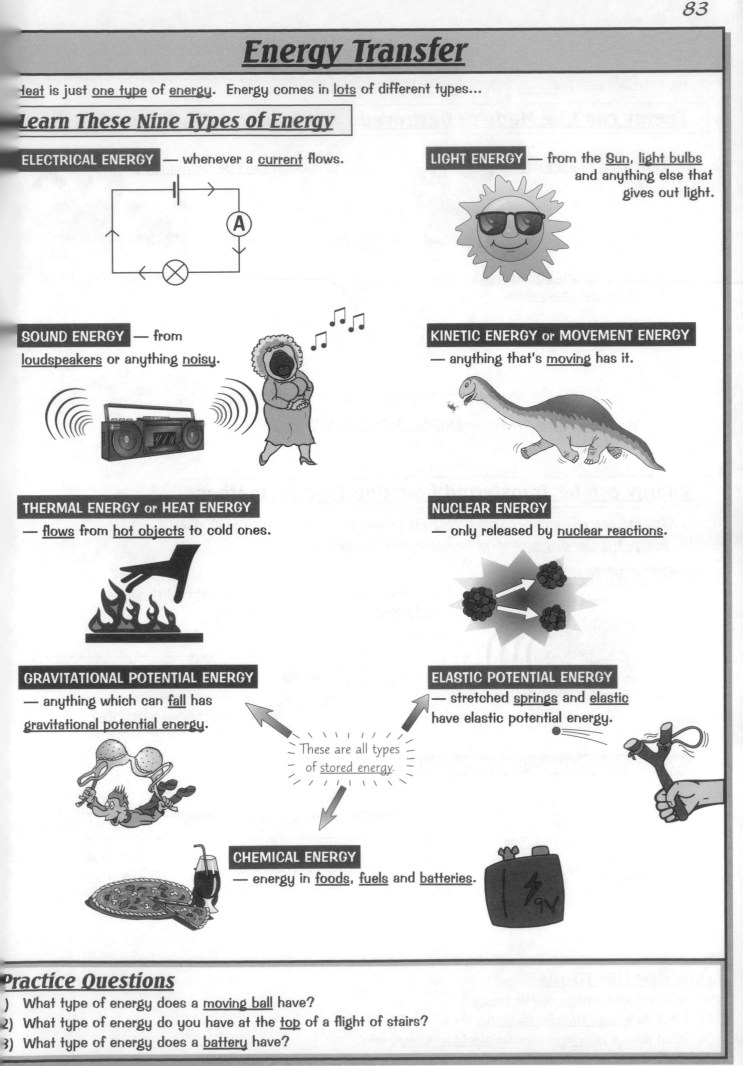

ELECTRICAL ENERGY — whenever a current flows.

LIGHT ENERGY — from the Sun, light bulbs and anything else that gives out light.

SOUND ENERGY — from loudspeakers or anything noisy.

KINETIC ENERGY or MOVEMENT ENERGY — anything that's moving has it.

THERMAL ENERGY or HEAT ENERGY — flows from hot objects to cold ones.

NUCLEAR ENERGY — only released by nuclear reactions.

GRAVITATIONAL POTENTIAL ENERGY — anything which can fall has gravitational potential energy.

ELASTIC POTENTIAL ENERGY — stretched springs and elastic have elastic potential energy.

These are all types of stored energy.

CHEMICAL ENERGY — energy in foods, fuels and batteries.

Practice Questions

1) What type of energy does a moving ball have?
2) What type of energy do you have at the top of a flight of stairs?
3) What type of energy does a battery have?

Energy Transfer

Ah, another page on <u>energy</u>. You've got to love them...

Energy can't be Made or Destroyed

1) Energy <u>can't be created</u>.

2) Energy <u>can't be destroyed</u>.

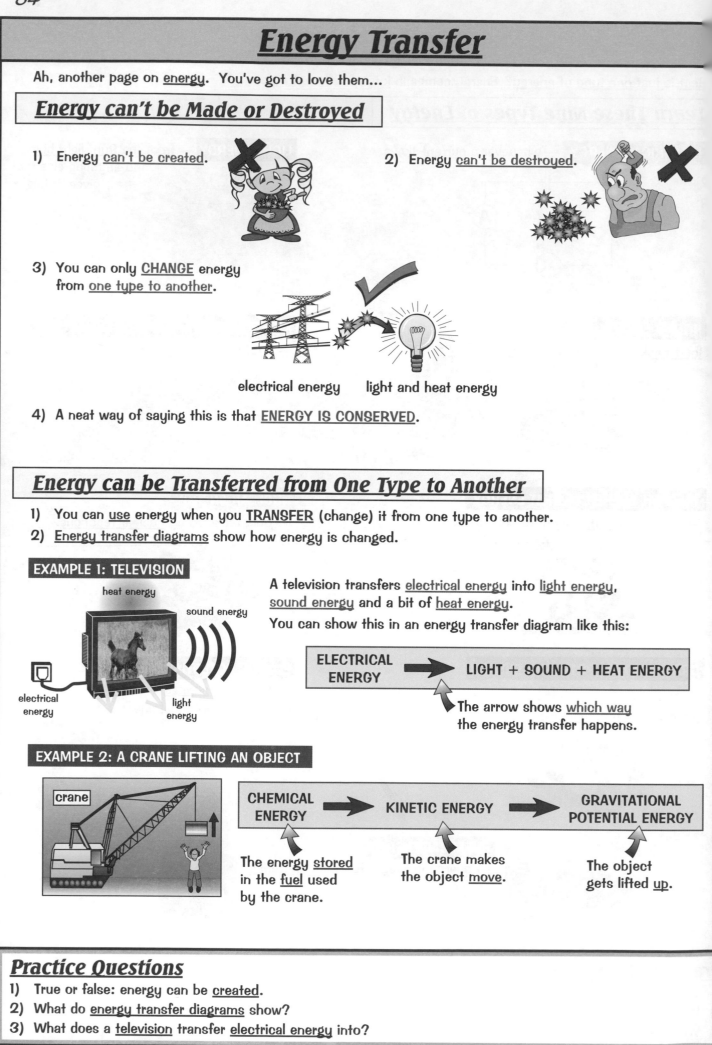

3) You can only <u>CHANGE</u> energy from <u>one type to another</u>.

electrical energy   light and heat energy

4) A neat way of saying this is that <u>ENERGY IS CONSERVED</u>.

Energy can be Transferred from One Type to Another

1) You can <u>use</u> energy when you <u>TRANSFER</u> (change) it from one type to another.

2) <u>Energy transfer diagrams</u> show how energy is changed.

EXAMPLE 1: TELEVISION

heat energy

sound energy

electrical energy

light energy

A television transfers <u>electrical energy</u> into <u>light energy</u>, <u>sound energy</u> and a bit of <u>heat energy</u>.

You can show this in an energy transfer diagram like this:

ELECTRICAL ENERGY → LIGHT + SOUND + HEAT ENERGY

The arrow shows <u>which way</u> the energy transfer happens.

EXAMPLE 2: A CRANE LIFTING AN OBJECT

crane

CHEMICAL ENERGY → KINETIC ENERGY → GRAVITATIONAL POTENTIAL ENERGY

The energy <u>stored</u> in the <u>fuel</u> used by the crane.

The crane makes the object <u>move</u>.

The object gets lifted <u>up</u>.

Practice Questions

1) True or false: energy can be <u>created</u>.
2) What do <u>energy transfer diagrams</u> show?
3) What does a <u>television</u> transfer <u>electrical energy</u> into?

Efficiency of Machines

Appliances are machines which transfer energy.
EFFICIENCY measures how much energy is transferred into useful energy.

Appliances Always Waste Energy

1) Appliances change energy from one type to another.

2) Some of the energy put in is transferred into useful types of energy.

3) Some of the energy put in is always transferred into types of energy that are NOT useful.

4) This energy is wasted.

Energy is Usually Wasted as Heat Energy

1) Some energy put in is always wasted as heat.

2) This is energy is transferred to the space around the appliance.

3) This makes the area around the appliance get warmer.

4) The wasted heat energy spreads out and can't be used.

Efficiency — How Much Energy is Transferred Usefully

There are two equations you can use to work out efficiency:

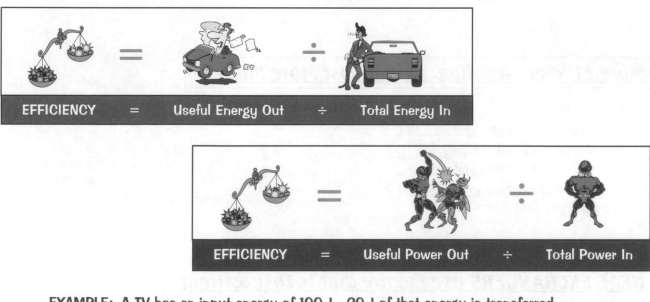

| EFFICIENCY | = | Useful Energy Out | ÷ | Total Energy In |

| EFFICIENCY | = | Useful Power Out | ÷ | Total Power In |

EXAMPLE: A TV has an input energy of 100 J. 20 J of that energy is transferred by the TV into useful energy. Work out the efficiency of the TV.

ANSWER: Use this energy efficiency equation:

Efficiency = useful energy out ÷ total energy in
= 20 ÷ 100
= 0.2 ⟵ You can leave your answer as a decimal, or you can turn it into a percentage.
All you need to do is multiply this by 100
0.2 × 100 = 20%

Practice Questions

What happens to energy that is not transferred usefully?

Write down two equations you can use to calculate efficiency.

Efficiency of Machines

By using _efficient_ devices, you can _cut down_ the amount of _energy_ you use to do something.

There are lots of Different ways to Save Energy in your Home

CHANGE THE LIGHT BULBS

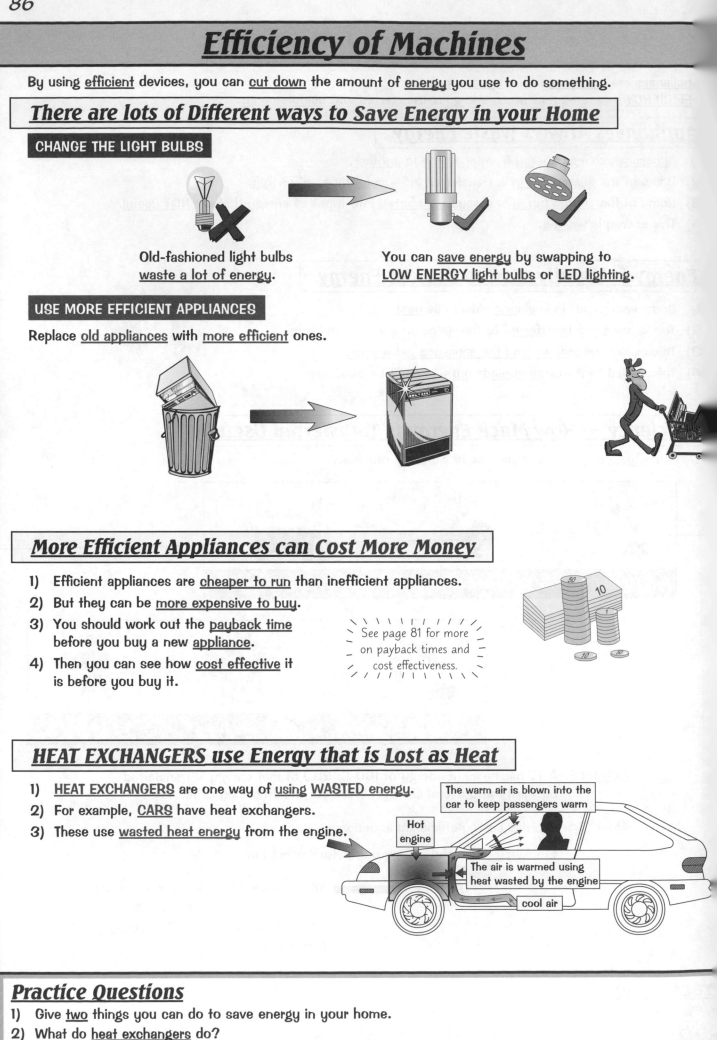

Old-fashioned light bulbs
waste a lot of energy.

You can _save energy_ by swapping to
LOW ENERGY light bulbs or **LED** lighting.

USE MORE EFFICIENT APPLIANCES

Replace _old appliances_ with _more efficient_ ones.

More Efficient Appliances can Cost More Money

1) Efficient appliances are _cheaper to run_ than inefficient appliances.

2) But they can be _more expensive to buy_.

3) You should work out the _payback time_ before you buy a new _appliance_.

4) Then you can see how _cost effective_ it is before you buy it.

See page 81 for more on payback times and cost effectiveness.

HEAT EXCHANGERS use Energy that is Lost as Heat

1) **HEAT EXCHANGERS** are one way of _using_ **WASTED** _energy_.

2) For example, **CARS** have heat exchangers.

3) These use _wasted heat energy_ from the engine.

The warm air is blown into the car to keep passengers warm

Hot engine

The air is warmed using heat wasted by the engine

cool air

Practice Questions

1) Give _two_ things you can do to save energy in your home.

2) What do _heat exchangers_ do?

Sankey Diagrams

ere's what <u>Sankey diagrams</u> are all about...

The Width of the Arrow Shows the Amount of Energy

1) SANKEY DIAGRAMS show you <u>how much</u> of the <u>input energy</u> is changed into different types of energy.

2) The <u>WIDER THE ARROW</u>, the <u>MORE ENERGY</u> it shows.

Example — TV:

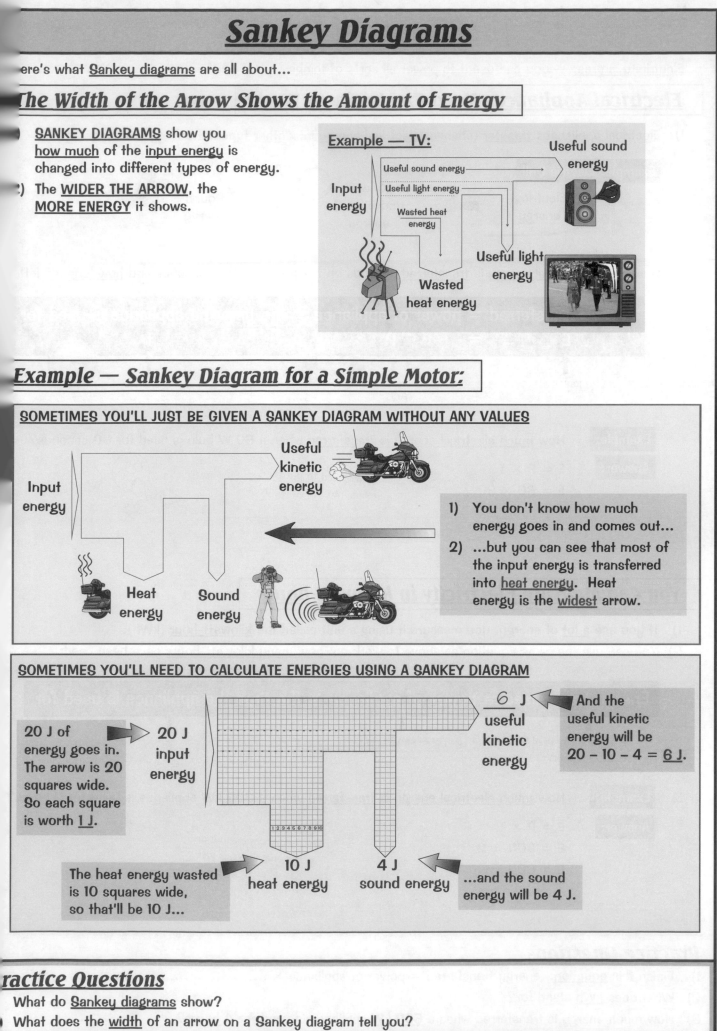

Example — Sankey Diagram for a Simple Motor:

SOMETIMES YOU'LL JUST BE GIVEN A SANKEY DIAGRAM WITHOUT ANY VALUES

Input energy

Useful kinetic energy

Heat energy

Sound energy

1) You don't know how much energy goes in and comes out...

2) ...but you can see that most of the input energy is transferred into <u>heat energy</u>. Heat energy is the <u>widest</u> arrow.

SOMETIMES YOU'LL NEED TO CALCULATE ENERGIES USING A SANKEY DIAGRAM

20 J of energy goes in. The arrow is 20 squares wide. So each square is worth <u>1 J</u>.

20 J input energy

<u>6</u> J useful kinetic energy

And the useful kinetic energy will be 20 − 10 − 4 = <u>6 J</u>.

The heat energy wasted is 10 squares wide, so that'll be 10 J...

10 J heat energy

4 J sound energy

...and the sound energy will be 4 J.

ractice Questions

What do <u>Sankey diagrams</u> show?

What does the <u>width</u> of an arrow on a Sankey diagram tell you?

Physics 1a — Energy

Electrical Energy

Electricity is great — you can use it to power all sorts of things.

Electrical Appliances Need Electricity to Work

1) Electrical appliances transfer (change) electrical energy into other types of energy (see page 83).

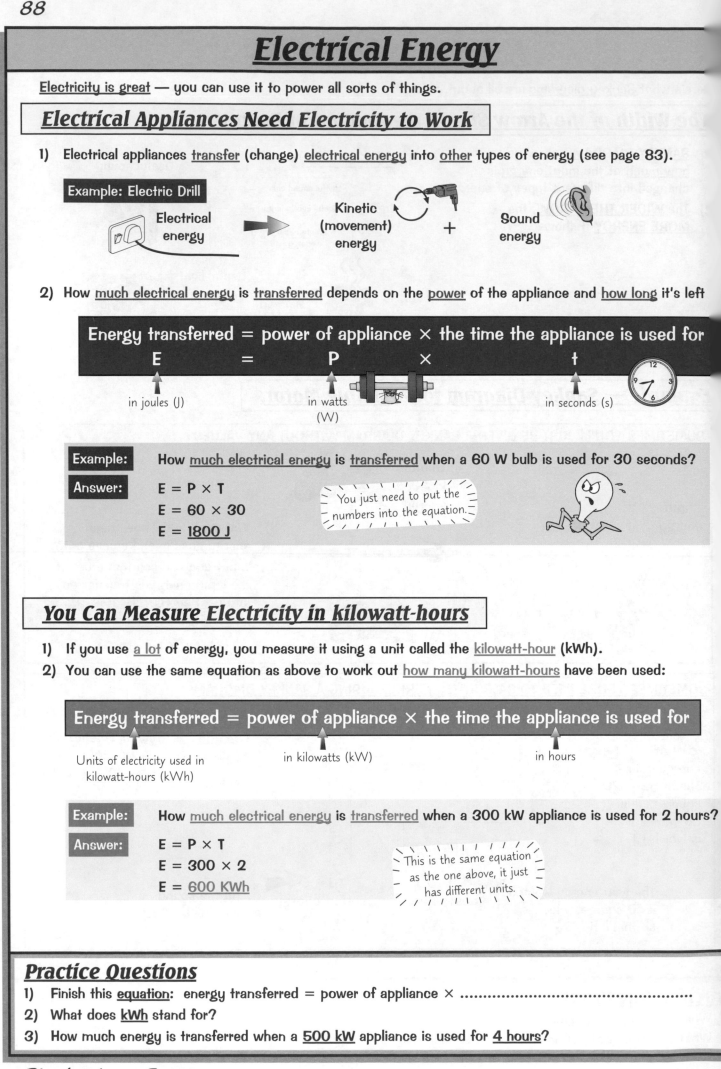

Example: Electric Drill

Electrical energy → Kinetic (movement) energy + Sound energy

2) How much electrical energy is transferred depends on the power of the appliance and how long it's left

Energy transferred = power of appliance × the time the appliance is used for

$$E = P \times t$$

in joules (J)   in watts (W)   in seconds (s)

Example: How much electrical energy is transferred when a 60 W bulb is used for 30 seconds?

Answer:
$E = P \times T$
$E = 60 \times 30$
$E = \underline{1800\ J}$

You just need to put the numbers into the equation.

You Can Measure Electricity in kilowatt-hours

1) If you use a lot of energy, you measure it using a unit called the kilowatt-hour (kWh).

2) You can use the same equation as above to work out how many kilowatt-hours have been used:

Energy transferred = power of appliance × the time the appliance is used for

Units of electricity used in kilowatt-hours (kWh)   in kilowatts (kW)   in hours

Example: How much electrical energy is transferred when a 300 kW appliance is used for 2 hours?

Answer:
$E = P \times T$
$E = 300 \times 2$
$E = \underline{600\ KWh}$

This is the same equation as the one above, it just has different units.

Practice Questions

1) Finish this equation: energy transferred = power of appliance × ....

2) What does kWh stand for?

3) How much energy is transferred when a 500 kW appliance is used for 4 hours?

Physics 1a — Energy

The Cost of Electricity

One of the bad things about electricity is that it <u>isn't free</u>...

You Can Use kilowatt-hours to Work out the Cost of Electricity

You can find the <u>total cost</u> of electricity using this equation:

TOTAL COST = Energy transferred (kWh) × **PRICE** per kWh

Example: Electricity costs 15p per kWh. How much does it cost to use 10 kWh?

Answer: <u>Total cost = Energy transferred (kWh) × price per kWh = 10 × 15 = 150p = £1.50</u>

Electricity Meters Show How Much Electricity You've Used

1) You can use <u>electricity meters</u> to work out <u>how much</u> electricity has been used.

2) For example, to work out how much electricity has been used in a week:

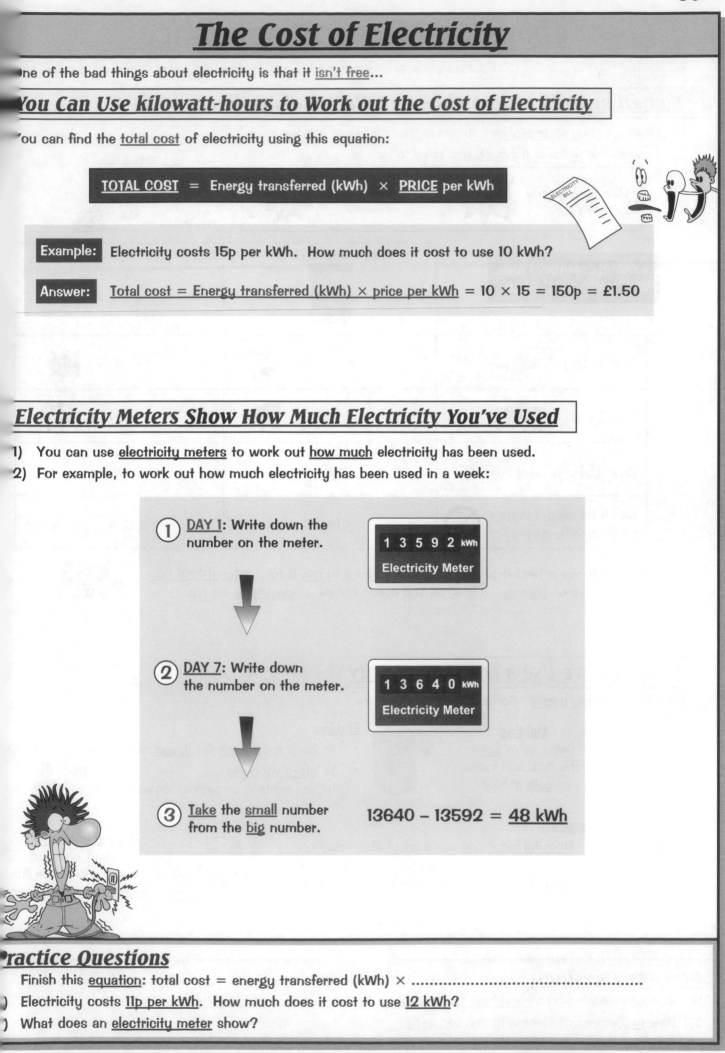

① <u>DAY 1</u>: Write down the number on the meter.

> 1 3 5 9 2 kWh
> **Electricity Meter**

② <u>DAY 7</u>: Write down the number on the meter.

> 1 3 6 4 0 kWh
> **Electricity Meter**

③ <u>Take</u> the <u>small</u> number from the <u>big</u> number.

13640 − 13592 = <u>48 kWh</u>

Practice Questions

Finish this <u>equation</u>: total cost = energy transferred (kWh) × ....

Electricity costs <u>11p per kWh</u>. How much does it cost to use <u>12 kWh</u>?

What does an <u>electricity meter</u> show?

Choosing Electrical Appliances

Sadly, this isn't about what <u>colour</u> MP3 player to get. But it is about choosing stuff...

Sometimes You Have a Choice of Electrical Appliances

1) When you buy an <u>appliance</u> you usually have a <u>few</u> to <u>choose</u> from.

2) To work out which is the <u>best</u>, you need to look at:

NEW IN!

The <u>good</u> points of each.

The <u>bad</u> points of each.

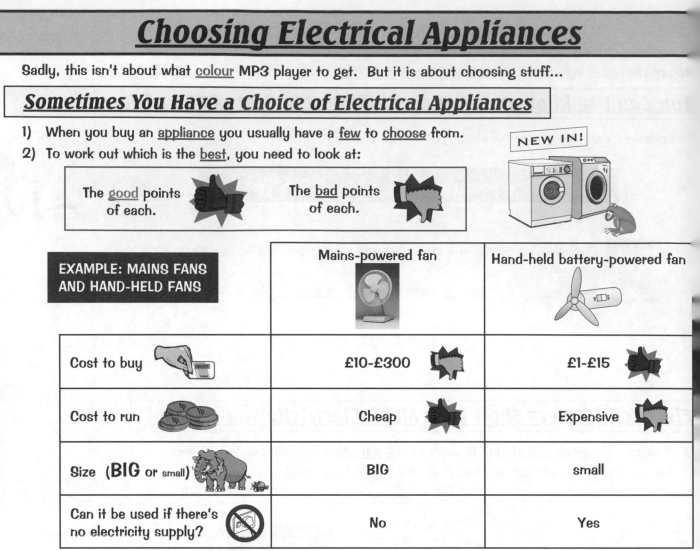

EXAMPLE: MAINS FANS AND HAND-HELD FANS	Mains-powered fan	Hand-held battery-powered fan
Cost to buy	£10-£300	£1-£15
Cost to run	Cheap	Expensive
Size (BIG or small)	BIG	small
Can it be used if there's no electricity supply?	No	Yes

3) Which appliance is best depends on what you want to <u>use</u> it for. A <u>hand-held fan</u> is <u>best</u> to take on <u>holiday</u>. It is <u>small</u> and doesn't need an <u>electricity</u> supply.

In the UK we Use a Lot of Electricity

Electricity is really <u>useful</u>. For example, we use it for:

<u>Lighting</u>:
Helps us to <u>see</u> in the dark and keeps us <u>safe</u> at night.

<u>Fridges</u>:
- To keep food <u>fresh</u> for <u>longer</u> so it's <u>safer</u> to eat.
- To <u>store vaccines</u> (which protect us against disease).

<u>Hospitals</u>:
- <u>Hospital machines</u> use a lot of electricity.
- Without electricity it can be hard to find out <u>what is wrong</u> with a patient or to <u>treat</u> them.

<u>Getting information</u>:
Without electricity we wouldn't have the <u>Internet</u> or <u>telephones</u>.

Practice Questions

1) Give <u>one</u> reason why a <u>hand-held fan</u> is the <u>best</u> fan to take on a <u>camping trip</u>.
2) Give <u>two</u> ways that electricity can be <u>useful</u>.

Physics 1a — Energy

Energy Sources & Power Stations

An <u>energy source</u> is something that you use to <u>make electricity</u>. They're <u>renewable</u> or <u>non-renewable</u>.

Non-Renewable Energy Sources Will Run Out One Day

The <u>non-renewable energy sources</u> are:

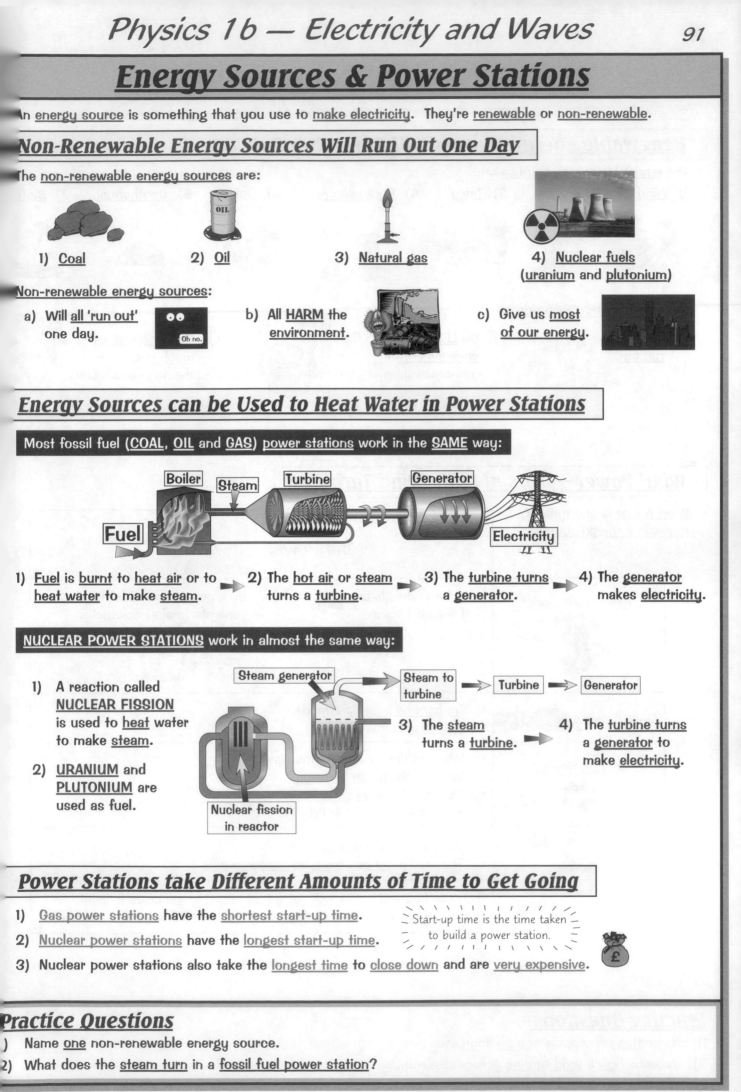

1) <u>Coal</u>

2) <u>Oil</u>

3) <u>Natural gas</u>

4) <u>Nuclear fuels</u>
(<u>uranium</u> and <u>plutonium</u>)

Non-renewable energy sources:

a) Will <u>all 'run out'</u> one day.

Oh no.

b) All <u>HARM</u> the environment.

c) Give us <u>most</u> of our energy.

Energy Sources can be Used to Heat Water in Power Stations

Most fossil fuel (<u>COAL</u>, <u>OIL</u> and <u>GAS</u>) power stations work in the <u>SAME</u> way:

Boiler Steam Turbine Generator

Fuel Electricity

1) <u>Fuel</u> is <u>burnt</u> to <u>heat air</u> or to <u>heat water</u> to make <u>steam</u>.

2) The <u>hot air</u> or <u>steam</u> turns a <u>turbine</u>.

3) The <u>turbine turns</u> a <u>generator</u>.

4) The <u>generator</u> makes <u>electricity</u>.

<u>NUCLEAR POWER STATIONS</u> work in almost the same way:

Steam generator Steam to turbine Turbine Generator

1) A reaction called <u>NUCLEAR FISSION</u> is used to <u>heat</u> water to make <u>steam</u>.

2) <u>URANIUM</u> and <u>PLUTONIUM</u> are used as fuel.

Nuclear fission in reactor

3) The <u>steam</u> turns a <u>turbine</u>.

4) The <u>turbine turns</u> a <u>generator</u> to make <u>electricity</u>.

Power Stations take Different Amounts of Time to Get Going

1) <u>Gas power stations</u> have the <u>shortest start-up time</u>.

2) <u>Nuclear power stations</u> have the <u>longest start-up time</u>.

Start-up time is the time taken to build a power station.

3) Nuclear power stations also take the <u>longest time</u> to <u>close down</u> and are <u>very expensive</u>.

Practice Questions

1) Name <u>one</u> non-renewable energy source.

2) What does the <u>steam turn</u> in a <u>fossil fuel power station</u>?

Renewable Energy Sources

Renewable energy sources will <u>not run out</u>. They also <u>don't</u> do too much <u>damage</u> to the Earth. Yay.

Renewable Energy Sources Will Never Run Out

See pages 93 to 96 for more on these.

The <u>renewable energy sources</u> are:

1) <u>Wind</u>   2) <u>Waves</u>   3) <u>Tides</u>   4) <u>Hydroelectric</u>   5) <u>Solar</u>   6) <u>Geothermal</u>   7) <u>Biofu</u>

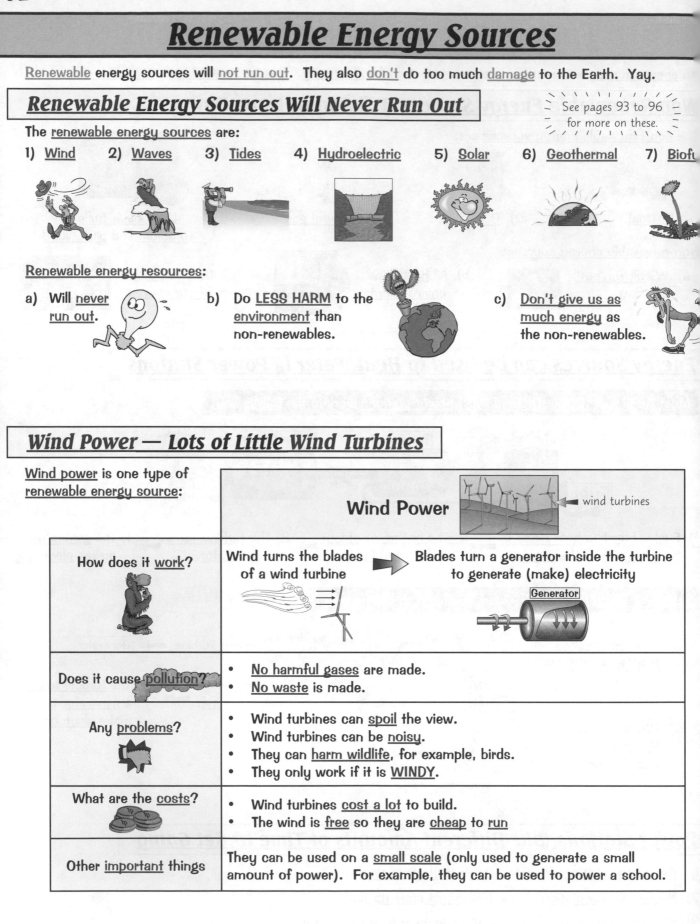

Renewable energy resources:

a) Will <u>never run out</u>.

b) Do <u>LESS HARM</u> to the <u>environment</u> than non-renewables.

c) <u>Don't give us as much energy</u> as the non-renewables.

Wind Power — Lots of Little Wind Turbines

Wind power is one type of renewable energy source:

Wind Power	wind turbines
How does it <u>work</u>?	Wind turns the blades of a wind turbine ➡ Blades turn a generator inside the turbine to generate (make) electricity
Does it cause <u>pollution</u>?	• <u>No harmful gases</u> are made. • <u>No waste</u> is made.
Any <u>problems</u>?	• Wind turbines can <u>spoil</u> the view. • Wind turbines can be <u>noisy</u>. • They can <u>harm wildlife</u>, for example, birds. • They only work if it is <u>WINDY</u>.
What are the <u>costs</u>?	• Wind turbines <u>cost a lot</u> to build. • The wind is <u>free</u> so they are <u>cheap</u> to <u>run</u>
Other <u>important</u> things	They can be used on a <u>small scale</u> (only used to generate a small amount of power). For example, they can be used to power a school.

Practice Questions

1) Name <u>three</u> renewable energy sources.

2) Describe <u>how</u> a <u>wind turbine</u> generates electricity.

Physics 1b — Electricity and Waves

Renewable Energy Sources

Solar cells are another renewable energy source — they're great when the Sun is shining.

Solar Cells — Expensive but Don't Harm the Environment

Solar cells generate (make) electricity from sunlight:

Solar Cells

How does it work?	Solar cells generate electricity from sunlight. SUNLIGHT → SOLAR CELL → ELECTRICITY
Does it cause pollution?	• No harmful gases are made. • No waste is made.
Any problems?	• They only work during the DAY and when it is SUNNY.
What are the costs?	• They cost a lot to make. • Sunlight is free so they are cheap to run.
Other important things	• They can be used on a small scale. For example, they can be used in small things like calculators. • They're useful in places that don't have mains electricity.

The National Grid Carries Electricity Around the Country

1) The National Grid is the name given to all the cables and other equipment that take electricity from power stations and carry it around the country.

2) Not everything that generates electricity can be connected to the National Grid.

There's more about the National Grid on page 99.

3) Some places only generate electricity on a small scale. It might cost too much to connect (join) these places to the National Grid.

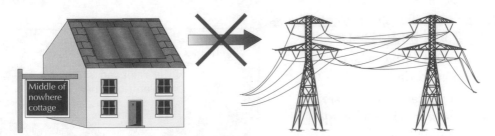

Middle of nowhere cottage

4) Some places are remote (in the middle of nowhere) and hard to get to. It might be too difficult to join these places to the National Grid.

Practice Questions

1) Write down two good things about using solar cells to generate electricity.

2) Why might a place that generates electricity not be part of the National Grid?

Renewable Energy Sources

We can use <u>moving water</u> to turn turbines and produce <u>electrical energy</u>. A big <u>high five</u> to water.

Hydroelectric Power Uses Falling Water

<u>Hydroelectric power</u> uses <u>falling water</u> to turn <u>turbines</u>:

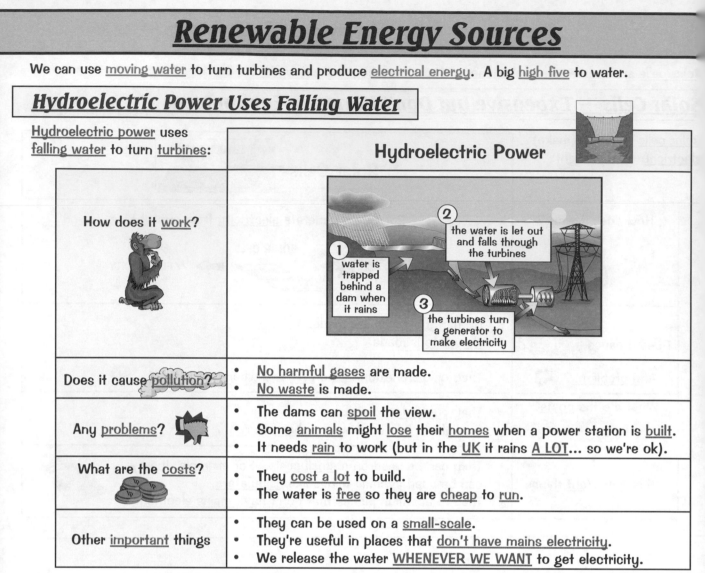

Hydroelectric Power

How does it <u>work</u>?	**1** water is trapped behind a dam when it rains **2** the water is let out and falls through the turbines **3** the turbines turn a generator to make electricity
Does it cause <u>pollution</u>?	• <u>No harmful gases</u> are made. • <u>No waste</u> is made.
Any <u>problems</u>?	• The dams can <u>spoil</u> the view. • Some <u>animals</u> might <u>lose</u> their <u>homes</u> when a power station is <u>built</u>. • It needs <u>rain</u> to work (but in the <u>UK</u> it rains <u>A LOT</u>... so we're ok).
What are the <u>costs</u>?	• They <u>cost a lot</u> to build. • The water is <u>free</u> so they are <u>cheap</u> to <u>run</u>.
Other <u>important</u> things	• They can be used on a <u>small-scale</u>. • They're useful in places that <u>don't have mains electricity</u>. • We release the water <u>WHENEVER WE WANT</u> to get electricity.

Pumped Storage Stores Energy Which Has Already Been Generated

1) We use <u>LESS ELECTRICITY</u> at <u>NIGHT</u>.

2) But most <u>power stations</u> make the <u>same amount</u> of electricity <u>all the time</u>.

3) This means <u>TOO MUCH</u> electricity is made at <u>night</u>.

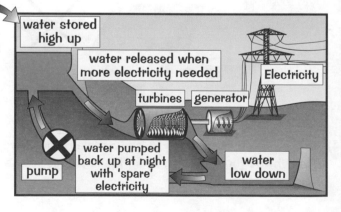

• Pumped storage uses the 'spare' <u>electricity</u> to <u>PUMP WATER</u> to a <u>HIGH UP</u> place.

• This water can be <u>RELEASED</u> when <u>lots of electricity</u> is needed.

• So <u>supply</u> (how much electricity there is) and <u>demand</u> (how much electricity is needed) can be matched.

water stored high up

water released when more electricity needed

Electricity

turbines generator

pump

water pumped back up at night with 'spare' electricity

water low down

Practice Questions

1) Write down <u>one</u> bad thing about <u>hydroelectric power</u>.

2) What is 'spare' electricity used for in <u>pumped storage</u>?

Renewable Energy Sources

Wave power and tidal power — they both use water, but they're VERY DIFFERENT. Oh yes.

Wave Power — Lots of Little Wave-Powered Turbines

Wave power uses the up and down motion of waves:

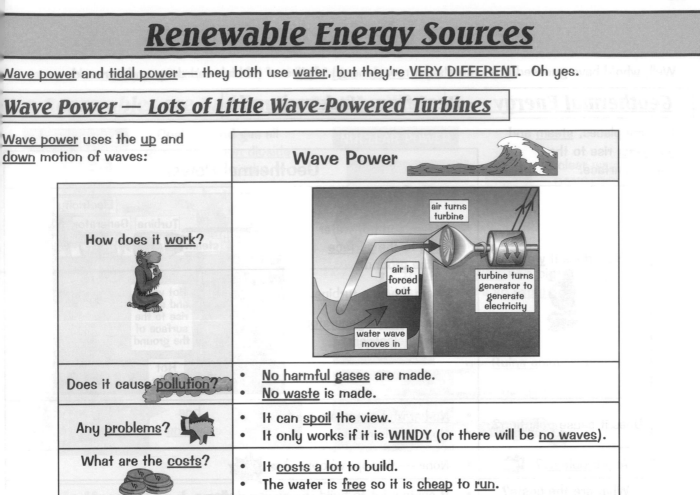

How does it work?	**Wave Power** — air turns turbine; air is forced out; turbine turns generator to generate electricity; water wave moves in
Does it cause pollution?	• No harmful gases are made. • No waste is made.
Any problems?	• It can spoil the view. • It only works if it is WINDY (or there will be no waves).
What are the costs?	• It costs a lot to build. • The water is free so it is cheap to run.

Tidal Power — Using the Tides to Generate Electricity

The tide can turn turbines:

How does it work?	The tide flows in ↓ As the tide flows out it turns turbines ↓ Turbines turn a generator to make electricity. **Tidal Power** — Tide flows out through the turbines; Tide held back
Does it cause pollution?	• No harmful gases are made. • No waste is made.
Any problems?	• It can spoil the view. • Some animals might lose their homes.
What are the costs?	• It costs a lot to build. • The water is free so it is cheap to run.
Other important things	• It can generate a lot of electricity • The tide always comes in twice a day — so we can rely on it.

Practice Questions

1) Give one advantage of using wave power.

2) Write down two problems with tidal power.

Comparison of Energy Sources

Here's a nice summary of the <u>good</u> and <u>bad</u> points of all the different energy sources.

<u>Can we Rely on Them to Give us Electricity?</u>

1) <u>NON-RENEWABLES</u> are <u>RELIABLE</u>.

2) <u>RENEWABLE</u> sources that use the <u>WEATHER</u> are <u>UNRELIABLE</u> in the UK.

Unreliable means we might not be able to get electricity from them when we need it.

<u>Set-Up Costs</u>

1) <u>Renewable</u> energy power stations <u>COST A LOT</u> to build.

2) <u>NUCLEAR</u> reactors and <u>HYDROELECTRIC dams</u> are the <u>MOST EXPENSIVE</u> to build.

<u>Time to Set-up and Take Apart</u>

1) <u>GAS power stations</u> have the <u>SHORTEST</u> start-up time of any fossil-fuel power station.

2) <u>NUCLEAR</u> power stations take the <u>LONGEST</u> to <u>take apart</u>.

<u>Running/Fuel Costs</u>

<u>RENEWABLES</u> are <u>CHEAP TO RUN</u> because the fuel is free.

Taking apart a power station is called decommissioning.

<u>Environmental Problems</u>

POLLUTION

Coal, Oil, Gas.

NOISE

Coal, Oil, Gas, Nuclear, Wind.

HARMS WILDLIFE

Hydroelectric, Tidal, Biofuels.

RUNNING OUT OF RESOURCES

Coal, Oil, Gas, Nuclear.

OTHER PROBLEMS

Nuclear (dangerous waste, explosions), Hydroelectric (dams bursting).

SPOILS VIEW

Coal, Oil, Gas, Nuclear, Tidal, Waves, Wind, Hydroelectric.

<u>Location</u>

A <u>power station</u> has to be <u>near</u> to the <u>stuff it runs on</u>.

COAL

Near <u>coal mines</u>

GEOTHERMAL

<u>Volcanic places</u>

HYDROELECTRIC

<u>Hilly</u>, <u>rainy places</u>

TIDAL

<u>End</u> of a <u>river</u>

WIND

<u>Windy</u> places

SOLAR and GAS

<u>Anywhere</u> in <u>UK</u>

WAVES

<u>On</u> or <u>near</u> the <u>COAST</u>

OIL

<u>Near</u> the <u>COAST</u>

NUCLEAR

<u>AWAY FROM PEOPLE</u> and <u>near WATER</u>

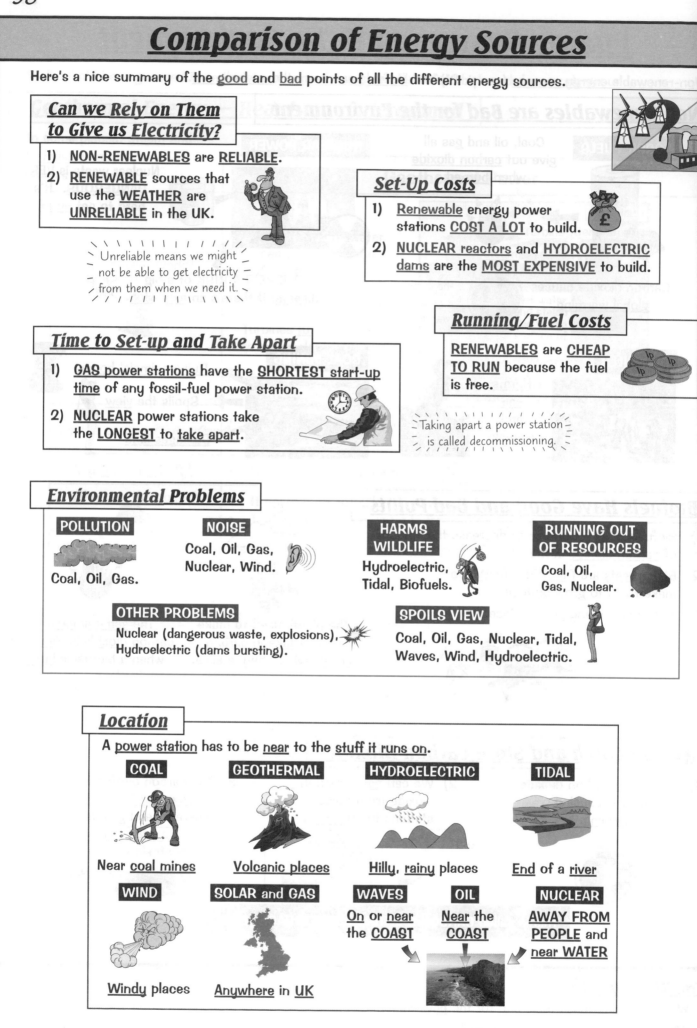

Electricity and the National Grid

It's the NATIONAL GRID that gets electricity to us from power stations. Thank you Mr National Grid.

The National Grid takes Electricity Around the UK

1) The National Grid is the name for all the stuff used to take electricity from power stations to where it's needed.

2) The electricity travels through the National Grid at a HIGH VOLTAGE and low current.

3) This helps cut down the energy that is lost as the electricity travels through the cables.

4) Here are all the bits and bobs that make the National Grid:

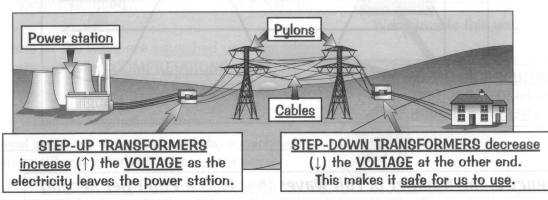

Power station

Pylons

Cables

STEP-UP TRANSFORMERS increase (↑) the **VOLTAGE** as the electricity leaves the power station.

STEP-DOWN TRANSFORMERS decrease (↓) the **VOLTAGE** at the other end. This makes it safe for us to use.

There are Different Ways to Transmit Electricity

1) Electrical energy can be moved around by OVERHEAD CABLES or UNDERGROUND CABLES.

2) Both have their good and bad points:

	Set-up cost	Need looking after?	Easy to get to (to fix)?	How it looks	Can weather damage them?	Can we rely on them?	Easy to set up?
Overhead Cables	Low	Lots	Yes	Ugly	Yes	less reliable	Yes
Underground Cables	High	Not much	No	Hidden	No	more reliable	No

Supply and Demand

1) Our energy demands keep on increasing. We want MORE AND MORE electricity.

2) To MEET THESE DEMANDS in the future:

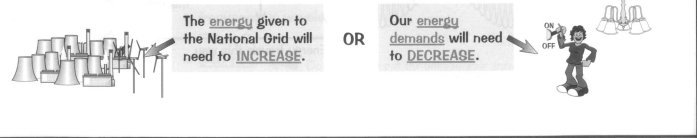

The energy given to the National Grid will need to INCREASE.

OR

Our energy demands will need to DECREASE.

Practice Questions

1) Do step-up transformers make voltage bigger or smaller?

2) Give one good thing about: a) overhead cables,   b) underground cables.

Wave Properties

When you look in a <u>mirror</u>, you see a <u>REFLECTION</u> of yourself.

Reflection of Light Lets Us See Things

1) We see stuff because light <u>REFLECTS</u> (bounces) off it into our <u>eyes</u>.

2) The <u>big thing</u> to remember for reflection is this:

> The angle of **INCIDENCE** is **ALWAYS** the same as the angle of **REFLECTION**.

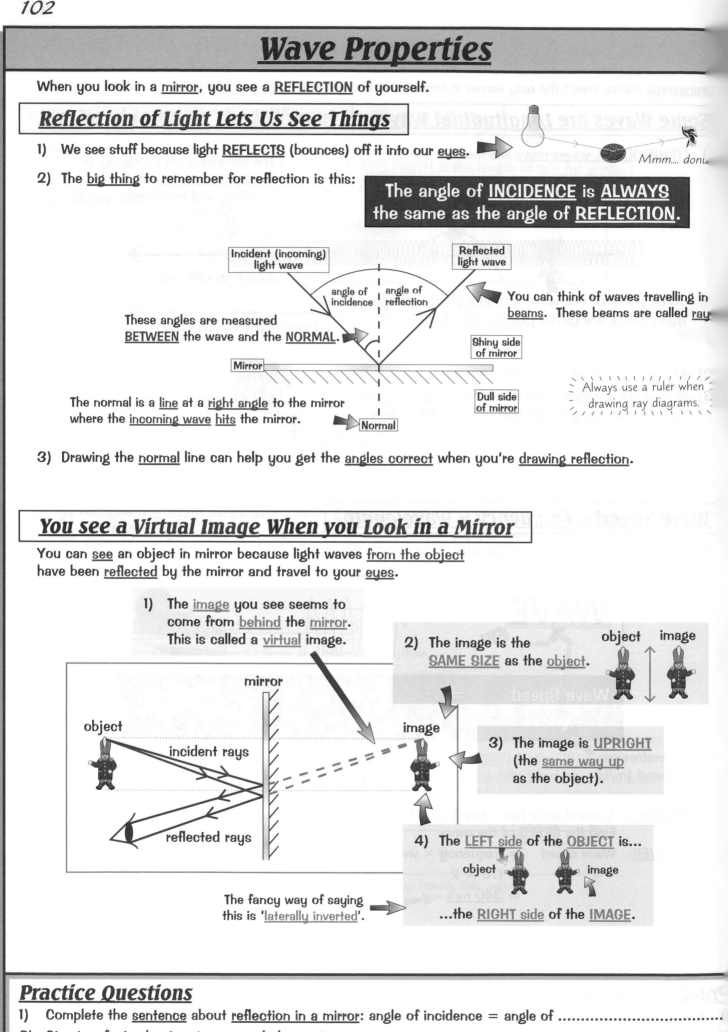

Mmm.... donu...

Incident (incoming) light wave

Reflected light wave

angle of incidence

angle of reflection

You can think of waves travelling in <u>beams</u>. These beams are called <u>ray</u>

These angles are measured <u>BETWEEN</u> the wave and the <u>NORMAL</u>.

Shiny side of mirror

Mirror

The normal is a <u>line</u> at a <u>right angle</u> to the mirror where the <u>incoming wave</u> <u>hits</u> the mirror.

Dull side of mirror

Normal

Always use a ruler when drawing ray diagrams.

3) Drawing the <u>normal</u> line can help you get the <u>angles correct</u> when you're <u>drawing reflection</u>.

You see a Virtual Image When you Look in a Mirror

You can <u>see</u> an object in mirror because light waves <u>from the object</u> have been <u>reflected</u> by the mirror and travel to your <u>eyes</u>.

1) The <u>image</u> you see seems to come from <u>behind</u> the <u>mirror</u>. This is called a <u>virtual</u> image.

2) The image is the <u>SAME SIZE</u> as the <u>object</u>.

object   image

mirror

object

incident rays

image

3) The image is <u>UPRIGHT</u> (the <u>same way up</u> as the object).

reflected rays

4) The <u>LEFT</u> side of the <u>OBJECT</u> is...

object   image

The fancy way of saying this is '<u>laterally inverted</u>'.

...the <u>RIGHT</u> side of the <u>IMAGE</u>.

Practice Questions

1) Complete the <u>sentence</u> about <u>reflection in a mirror</u>: angle of incidence = angle of ....

2) Give <u>two</u> facts about an <u>image</u> made by a <u>mirror</u>.

Refraction and Diffraction

s well as being reflected, waves can <u>SPREAD OUT</u> and <u>BEND</u>.

Diffraction — Waves Spreading Out

The wave <u>SPREADS OUT</u> at as it <u>passes</u> through the <u>gap</u>.

1) All waves <u>SPREAD OUT</u> (<u>diffract</u>) when they pass through a <u>gap</u>.

2) <u>HOW MUCH</u> they spread out depends on the <u>SIZE of the gap</u> compared to the <u>WAVELENGTH</u> of the wave:

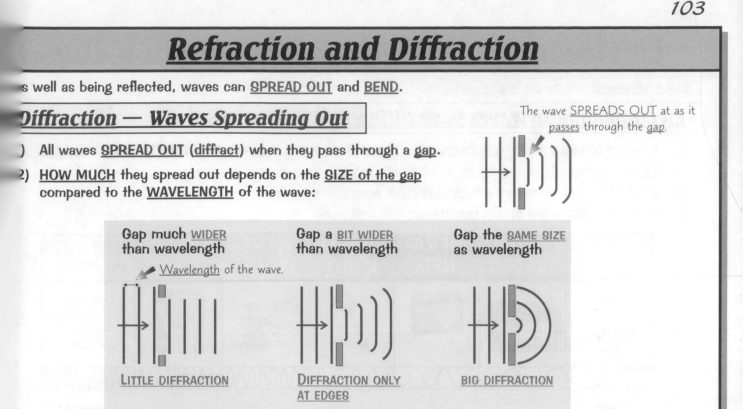

Refraction — Waves Changing Direction

1) When a wave <u>moves</u> from <u>one material</u> to <u>another</u>, it can <u>change direction</u>.

2) This <u>change in direction</u> is called <u>REFRACTION</u>.

3) Waves will <u>only</u> be <u>refracted</u> if they meet a new material <u>at an angle</u>.

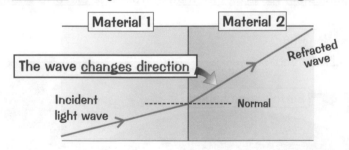

4) If a wave travelling <u>along the normal</u> meets a new material, it will <u>NOT refract</u>.

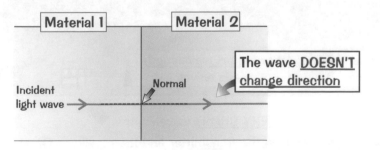

Practice Questions

1) Do waves <u>diffract</u> or <u>refract</u> when they <u>pass</u> through a gap?

2) Will a light wave travelling along a normal <u>refract</u>?

Electromagnetic Waves and Communication

Electromagnetic waves are <u>really useful</u> to us. Here is more about them...

Electromagnetic Waves have Different Wavelengths

1) There are <u>SEVEN</u> types of <u>electromagnetic wave</u>. They all have <u>different WAVELENGTHS</u> and <u>FREQUEN</u>
2) <u>ALL</u> electromagnetic waves travel at the <u>SAME SPEED</u> in a <u>vacuum</u>, like <u>space</u>.
3) <u>ALL</u> electromagnetic waves are <u>TRANSVERSE</u> waves (see p. 100).
4) The seven types make up the <u>electromagnetic spectrum</u>:

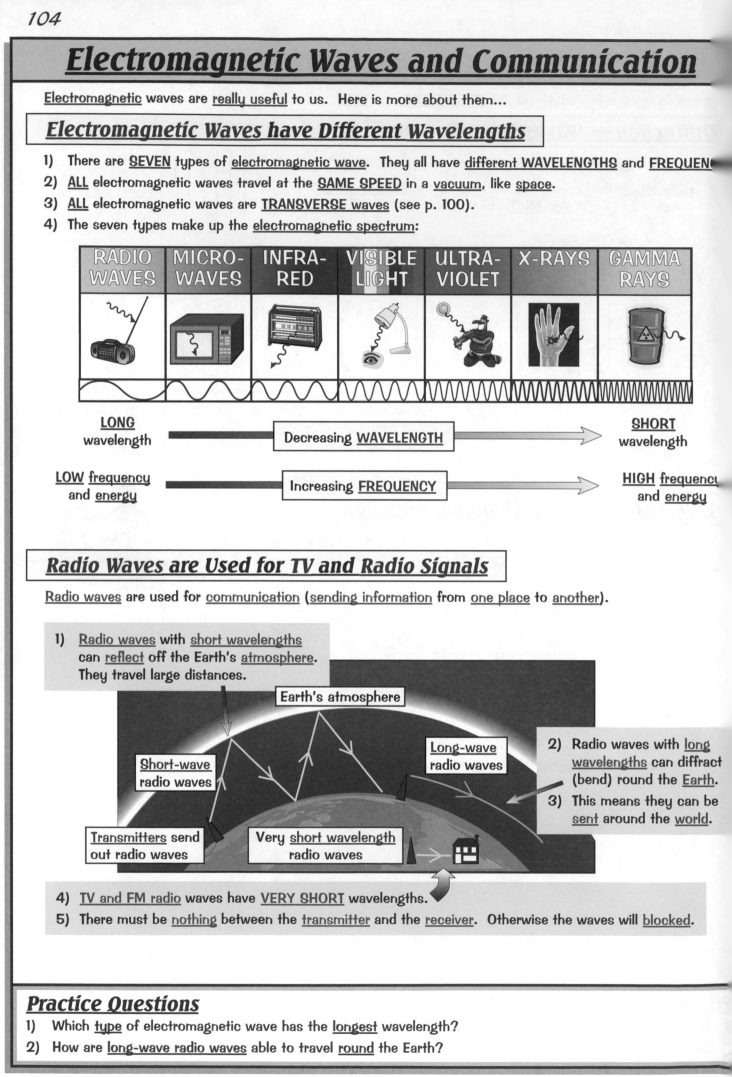

| RADIO WAVES | MICRO-WAVES | INFRA-RED | VISIBLE LIGHT | ULTRA-VIOLET | X-RAYS | GAMMA RAYS |

LONG wavelength ← Decreasing **WAVELENGTH** → **SHORT** wavelength

LOW frequency and energy ← Increasing **FREQUENCY** → **HIGH** frequency and energy

Radio Waves are Used for TV and Radio Signals

<u>Radio waves</u> are used for <u>communication</u> (<u>sending information</u> from <u>one place</u> to <u>another</u>).

1) <u>Radio waves</u> with <u>short wavelengths</u> can <u>reflect</u> off the Earth's <u>atmosphere</u>. They travel large distances.

Earth's atmosphere

Long-wave radio waves

Short-wave radio waves

Transmitters send out radio waves

Very short wavelength radio waves

2) Radio waves with <u>long wavelengths</u> can diffract (bend) round the <u>Earth</u>.

3) This means they can be <u>sent</u> around the <u>world</u>.

4) <u>TV and FM radio</u> waves have <u>VERY SHORT</u> wavelengths.
5) There must be <u>nothing</u> between the <u>transmitter</u> and the <u>receiver</u>. Otherwise the waves will <u>blocked</u>.

Practice Questions

1) Which <u>type</u> of electromagnetic wave has the <u>longest</u> wavelength?
2) How are <u>long-wave radio waves</u> able to travel <u>round</u> the Earth?

Electromagnetic Waves and Their Uses

Radio waves aren't the only waves used for communication...

Microwaves are Used to Send Satellite Television Signals

2) The signal is picked up by the SATELLITE.

3) The satellite sends the signal back to Earth in a DIFFERENT direction.

1) The microwave signal is sent from a TRANSMITTER into space.

4) The signal is picked up by a SATELLITE DISH on the ground.

Microwaves are Also Used by Mobile Phones

1) Mobile phone signals travel as microwaves between your phone and the nearest transmitter.

2) Some types of microwaves are ABSORBED (taken in) by cells and can heat them up.

3) Some people think using your mobile phone a lot is dangerous. The worry is that the microwaves COULD heat and damage the cells in your body.

4) BUT there ISN'T any proof that mobile phones are dangerous.

Infrared Waves are Used for Remote Controls

Infrared waves are used in wireless remote controllers, such as TV remotes.

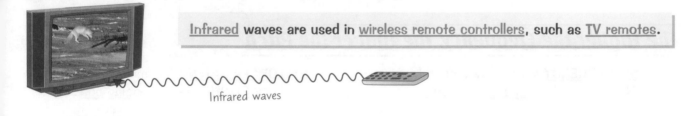

Infrared waves

Visible Light is Used in Photography

1) Cameras use visible light to take photographs.

2) A camera focuses light on a film or a sensor at the back of the camera.

3) The film or sensor records an image.

Practice Questions

1) What type of electromagnetic waves do mobile phones use?

2) Give one use of infrared radiation.

Smile for the camera.

Sound Waves

We hear sounds after <u>vibrations</u> reach our <u>ears</u>...

Sound Travels as a Wave

1) <u>Sound waves</u> are a type of <u>longitudinal wave</u> (see page 101).

2) They cause <u>vibrations</u> in the material they travel in.

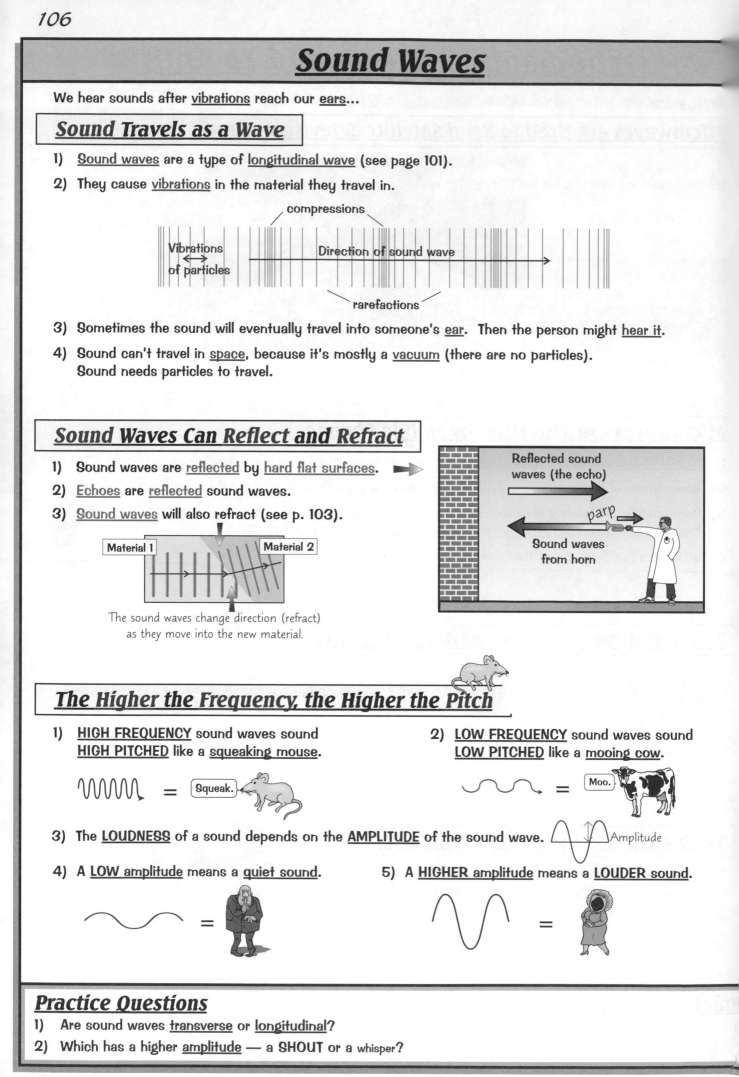

compressions

Vibrations of particles

Direction of sound wave

rarefactions

3) Sometimes the sound will eventually travel into someone's <u>ear</u>. Then the person might <u>hear it</u>.

4) Sound can't travel in <u>space</u>, because it's mostly a <u>vacuum</u> (there are no particles). Sound needs particles to travel.

Sound Waves Can Reflect and Refract

1) Sound waves are <u>reflected</u> by <u>hard flat surfaces</u>.

2) <u>Echoes</u> are <u>reflected</u> sound waves.

3) <u>Sound waves</u> will also refract (see p. 103).

Material 1   Material 2

The sound waves change direction (refract) as they move into the new material.

Reflected sound waves (the echo)

parp

Sound waves from horn

The Higher the Frequency, the Higher the Pitch

1) **HIGH FREQUENCY** sound waves sound **HIGH PITCHED** like a <u>squeaking mouse</u>.

= Squeak.

2) **LOW FREQUENCY** sound waves sound **LOW PITCHED** like a <u>mooing cow</u>.

= Moo.

3) The <u>**LOUDNESS**</u> of a sound depends on the <u>**AMPLITUDE**</u> of the sound wave. Amplitude

4) A <u>LOW</u> amplitude means a <u>quiet sound</u>.

=

5) A <u>**HIGHER**</u> amplitude means a <u>**LOUDER**</u> sound.

=

Practice Questions

1) Are sound waves <u>transverse</u> or <u>longitudinal</u>?

2) Which has a higher <u>amplitude</u> — a **SHOUT** or a whisper?

The Doppler Effect and Red-shift

The Doppler effect and red-shift sound a bit scary. But take it slowly and it'll all make sense.

Wavelength and Frequency seem to Change if the Wave Source Moves

1) A wave source is anything that emits (gives out) waves.

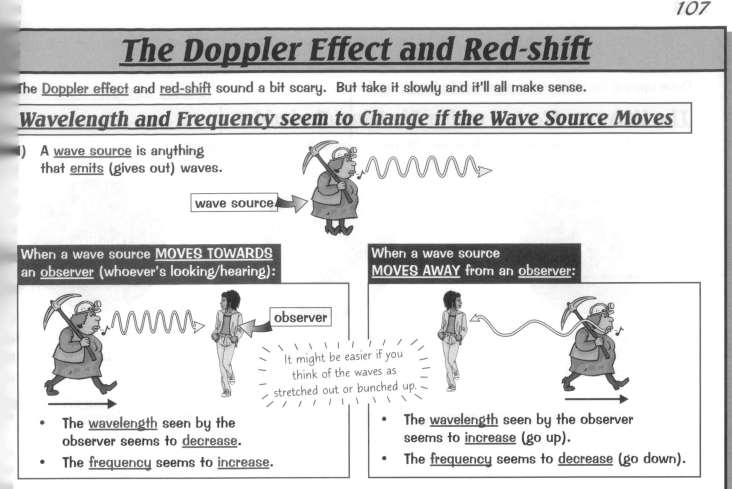

When a wave source **MOVES TOWARDS** an observer (whoever's looking/hearing):

observer

It might be easier if you think of the waves as stretched out or bunched up.

When a wave source **MOVES AWAY** from an observer:

- The wavelength seen by the observer seems to decrease.
- The frequency seems to increase.

- The wavelength seen by the observer seems to increase (go up).
- The frequency seems to decrease (go down).

2) This is called the **DOPPLER EFFECT**.
3) The Doppler effect can happen to light waves, sound waves and microwaves.

Distant Galaxies are Moving Away From Us

1) A galaxy is a group of stars.
2) The wavelength of light from **DISTANT GALAXIES** is longer than it should be.
3) The wavelength is longer because the galaxies are moving away from us.
4) The longer the wavelength, the redder the light looks. That's why this effect is called **RED-SHIFT**.

The Further Away a Galaxy is, the Greater the Red-shift

1) There are millions of galaxies in the universe.
2) The further away the galaxy is, the more the light is red-shifted.
3) So, distant galaxies are moving away from us **FASTER** than the nearer ones.
4) This is evidence (signs) that the universe is **EXPANDING** (getting bigger).

Bye

Practice Questions

1) The longer the wavelength of light gets, the redder it looks. What is this effect called?
2) True or false: the universe is shrinking.

Answers

Biology 1b — Environment and Evolution

Page 31 — Adaptations

1) It's got features that help it to survive there.
2) Any two from: long thin shape / thin coat of fur / very little body fat / sandy colour
3) Any two from: round shape / thick coat of fur / lots of body fat / white fur

Page 32 — Adaptations

1) Any two from: thick stem / spines / long roots
2) thorns
3) Any one from: hot volcanoes / at the bottom of the sea / salty lakes

Page 33 — Competition and Environmental Change

1) Any two from: light / nutrients / water / space
2) Any two from: food / mates / space

Page 34 — Measuring Environmental Change

1) a rain gauge
2) The air is clean.
3) The water is dirty.

Page 35 — Pyramids of Biomass

1) the seaweed

Page 36 — Energy Transfer and Decay

1) the Sun
2) Energy is lost as heat. Energy is lost in waste products.

Page 37 — The Carbon Cycle

1) true
2) photosynthesis
3) respiration, combustion (burning)

Page 38 — Genes and Chromosomes

1) chromosomes
2) false — Different genes control your eye colour and your hair colour.
3) your parents

Page 39 — Variation

1) true
2) eye colour
3) height of a plant

Page 40 — Reproduction

1) sperm
2) two
3) the same

Page 41 — Cloning

1) false — Clones have exactly the same genes as each other.
2) taking cuttings, tissue culture

Page 42 — Cloning

1) Take the nucleus out of an egg cell.
2) Any one from: You can make lots of copies of a perfect plant or animal. / Studying clones might help us understa some diseases.
3) Any one from: Clones have the same genes. This means a new disease could kill a group of clones all at once. / Cloned animals might not be as healthy as normal ones.

Page 43 — Genetic Engineering

1) enzymes
2) Any one from: You can add vitamins to GM crops. / GM cr have a higher yield than normal crops. This means we get more food from GM crops.
3) Any one from: GM crops could affect the number of flowe and insects nearby. / Some people think GM crops are no safe to eat.

Page 44 — Evolution

1) simple
2) Evolution means that living things change over time.
3) false — Similar organisms are related.

Page 45 — Natural Selection and Mutations

1) Charles Darwin
2) true
3) a change in a gene

Page 46 — More About Evolution

1) Lamarck
2) because there is lots of evidence for it
3) Any two from: It went against the Church who thought tha life on Earth was made by God. / Darwin couldn't explain ho new features appeared. He also couldn't explain how they were passed on. / There wasn't much evidence. This meant most scientists weren't sure he was right.

Chemistry 1a — Products from Rocks

Page 47 — Atoms and Elements

1) protons and neutrons
2) positive
3) about 100

Page 48 — The Periodic Table

1) groups
2) false — All of the elements in a group have the same numbe of electrons in their outer shells.

Page 49 — Electron Shells

1) the inside shell
2) 2, 8, 8

Page 50 — Compounds and Chemical Reactions

1) by sharing electrons
2) 5 g

Answers

e 51 — *Limestone*

It's quarried.

It thermally decomposes into calcium oxide and carbon dioxide.

salt, water and carbon dioxide

e 52 — *Limestone*

The limewater goes cloudy.

Limestone is heated with clay.

e 53 — *Using Limestone*

Any two from: noise and pollution / ugly hole / ugly tips / destroys the homes of birds and animals

Any three from: they're cheap. / Limestone is easy to cut. / Concrete is easy to shape. / They don't rust or rot.

e 54 — *Getting Metals from Rocks*

A compound with a lot of metal in it.

yes

e 55 — *Getting Metals from Rocks*

true

purifying copper and extracting metals

e 56 — *Getting Metals from Rocks*

yes

Plants are grown in soil that has copper in it.

The plants take up the copper.

The plants are burnt. You get the copper out of the ash.

ge 57 — *Impacts of Extracting Metals*

a) Any one from: metals to make things with. / Brings money into the area. / Jobs in the mine.

b) Any one from: ugly and noisy. / Destroys the homes of animals and birds. / People can fall down old mines.

Any three from: less rubbish. / Saves energy and fossil fuels. / Less pollution. / Saves money. / Stops metals running out so fast.

ge 58 — *Properties of Metals*

Any two from: strong / bendy / great at conducting heat and electricity

It can be bent, but is hard enough to make water pipes and tanks. It doesn't react with water.

age 59 — *Alloys*

) It's brittle.

) An alloy is a mixture of two or more metals. Or it can be a mixture of a metal and a non-metal.

age 60 — *Fractional Distillation of Crude Oil*

) carbon and hydrogen

) A mixture has two or more different elements or compounds in it. There are no chemical bonds between the elements or compounds.

) fractional distillation

Page 61 — *Properties and Uses of Crude Oil*

1) methane, ethane, propane, butane

2) viscous, high boiling point, hard to set on fire

Page 62 — *Using Crude Oil as a Fuel*

1) Any one from: fuels / making medicines

2) no

3) Birds get covered in the oil and are poisoned. Sea creatures are also poisoned.

Page 63 — *Environmental Problems*

1) Any two from: water vapour / sulfur dioxide / oxides of nitrogen / carbon dioxide / carbon monoxide

2) sulfur dioxide and oxides of nitrogen

Page 64 — *More Environmental Problems*

1) carbon dioxide

2) Any two from: takes energy to make. / Cars need a special engine to use it. / Hard to store.

Chemistry 1b — Oils, Earth and Atmosphere

Page 65 — *Cracking Crude Oil*

1) smaller

2) short alkanes and alkenes

3) Any one from: heat them so that they vaporise and then pass the gas over a hot catalyst. / Heat them so that they vaporise and then mix the gas with steam at a very high temperature.

Page 66 — *Alkenes and Ethanol*

1) It turns from orange to colourless.

2) renewable

Page 67 — *Using Alkenes to Make Polymers*

1) monomers

2) Any three from: waterproof coatings / tooth fillings / plasters / mattresses made of memory foam / plastic bags that can biodegrade.

Page 68 — *Plant Oils*

1) The olives are crushed. The oil is then pressed out of the olive mush. Water and other unwanted things can then be removed from the oil.

2) Any two from: they have higher boiling points than water so they cook foods faster and at higher temperatures. / They give food a different flavour. / They give food more energy.

Page 69 — *Plant Oils*

1) They have lots of energy in them.

2) carbon=carbon double bonds

3) false — Eating unsaturated oils gives you a lower risk of heart disease than saturated oils.

Answers

Page 70 — Emulsions

1) an emulsion
2) to stop emulsions separating out

Page 71 — Continental Drift

1) true
2) Any one from: Wegener didn't have much evidence that he was right. / Some of Wegener's sums didn't add up. / Most people thought the continents used to be joined together by land bridges.

Page 72 — The Earth's Structure

1) because of convection currents in the mantle
2) volcanoes and earthquakes

Page 73 — The Atmosphere

1) 80%
2) Water vapour from volcanoes condensed.

Physics 1a — Energy

Page 74 — Infrared Radiation

1) a hot object
2) true
3) black

Page 75 — Solids, Liquids and Gases

1) true
2) false — Particles in a gas have more energy than particles in a liquid.

Page 76 — Conduction

1) false — Heat energy travels slowly through insulators.
2) free electrons

Page 77 — Convection

1) the amount of stuff you have in a certain volume
2) false — Hot fluids will move above cold fluids.

Page 78 — Condensation and Evaporation

1) Any two from: raise the temperature / make the surface area bigger / increase the airflow over the liquid
2) Condensation is when a gas changes to a liquid.

Page 79 — Rate of Heat Transfer

1) true
2) so they can transfer heat quickly

Page 80 — Rate of Heat Transfer

1) reduce heat transfer
2) to help them lose heat by radiation and keep cool

Page 81 — Energy Efficiency in the Home

1) to reduce heat loss
2) The time it takes to save the amount of money you spent. The initial cost ÷ the annual saving on heating bills.

Page 82 — Specific Heat Capacity

1) the amount of energy needed to raise the temperature of 1 kg of a substance by 1 °C
2) Energy = mass × specific heat capacity × temperature change
   $E = m \times c \times \theta$

Page 83 — Energy Transfer

1) kinetic energy
2) gravitational potential energy
3) chemical energy

Page 84 — Energy Transfer

1) false — Energy can never be created or destroyed. It can only be changed from one form to another.
2) how energy can be changed from one form to another
3) light energy, sound energy and heat energy

Page 85 — Efficiency of Machines

1) It is wasted, usually as heat energy.
2) Efficiency = useful energy out ÷ total energy in
   Efficiency = useful power out ÷ total power in

Page 86 — Efficiency of Machines

1) change the light bulbs / use more efficient appliances
2) Heat exchangers use energy that is lost as heat.

Page 87 — Sankey Diagrams

1) Sankey diagrams show how much of the input energy is changed into different types of energy.
2) how much energy there is

Page 88 — Electrical Energy

1) the time the appliance is used for
2) kilowatt-hours
3) $E = P \times t$
   $= 500 \times 4$
   $= 2000$ kWh

Page 89 — The Cost of Electricity

1) price per kWh
2) total cost = energy transferred × price per kWh
   $= 12 \times 11$
   $= 132p = £1.32$
3) It shows how much electricity you've used.

Page 90 — Choosing Electrical Appliances

1) Any one from: cheap to buy / small / can be used in places without electricity
2) Any two from: lighting to keep us safe at night / fridges to keep food fresh / fridges to store vaccines / hospital machines.

Answers

...ysics 1b — Electricity and Waves

...e 91 — Energy Sources & Power Stations

Any one from: coal / oil / natural gas / nuclear fuels

a turbine

...e 92 — Renewable Energy Sources

Any one from: wind / waves / tides / hydroelectric / solar / geothermal / biofuels

Wind turns the blades of the wind turbine, which turns a generator inside the turbine to generate electricity.

...e 93 — Renewable Energy Sources

Any two from: solar panels don't cause pollution / they're cheap to run / they can be used on a small scale / they are useful in places without mains electricity.

It might cost too much or be too difficult to join the place to the National Grid.

...e 94 — Renewable Energy Sources

Any one from: hydroelectric dams can spoil the view / some animals might lose their homes when a power station is built / they need rain to work / they cost a lot to build

to pump water high up so it can be released when lots of electricity is needed

...ge 95 — Renewable Energy Sources

Any one from: it produces no harmful gases and no waste / it is cheap to run

Any two from: it can spoil the view / some animals might lose their homes / it costs a lot to build

...ge 96 — Renewable Energy Sources

Any one from: no harmful gases are made / no waste is made / it's cheap to run (steam and hot water is free).

Biofuels are burnt to heat up water to produce steam.

...age 97 — Energy Sources and the Environment

Any one from: they give out carbon dioxide / they cause global warming.

into holes under the North sea where gas and oil used to be

...age 99 — Electricity and the National Grid

bigger

a) Any one from: low set-up cost / easy to get to / easy to set up.

b) Any one from: don't need much looking after / hidden so they don't spoil the view / can't be damaged by the weather / reliable.

...age 100 — Wave Basics

) up and down

) light waves

...age 101 — Wave Basics

) sound waves

) wave speed = frequency × wavelength

Page 102 — Wave Properties

1) reflection

2) Any two from: the image will be virtual / it will be upright / it will be the same size as the object / it will be laterally inverted — the left side will be the right side.

Page 103 — Refraction and Diffraction

1) diffract

2) no

Page 104 — Electromagnetic Waves and Communication

1) radio waves

2) They can diffract (bend) around the Earth.

Page 105 — Electromagnetic Waves and Their Uses

1) microwaves

2) wireless remote controllers

Page 106 — Sound Waves

1) longitudinal

2) a shout (it is louder)

Page 107 — The Doppler Effect and Red-shift

1) red-shift

2) false — The universe is expanding.

Page 108 — How the Universe Started

1) an explosion that made the universe expand

2) cosmic microwave background radiation

Index

Index